MIND GROWING

**LEADERSHIP
BUILD THRIVING
COMPANIES THROUGH
PERSONAL GROWTH**

MARC VANSCHOENWINKEL

DEDICATION

I want to dedicate this book to the institution and the professor that changed my intellectual thinking and life forever. The inspiration I got from the Free University of Brussels and, more specifically, from Professor Dr. Jean-Pierre De Waele shaped my mind in an amazing way. I hope I will do right by them in writing this book.

"Thought must never submit, neither to a dogma, nor to a party, nor to a passion, nor to an interest, nor to a preconceived idea, nor to whatever it may be, only to the facts themselves, because, for thought, submission would mean ceasing to be."

Henry Poincaré

First Printing, 2020

ISBN 978-1-78972-856-9

www.mindgrowing.net

MIND GR○WING

TABLE OF CONTENTS

PREFACE

What is 'mind growing'?

The mind is the element that enables a person to be aware of the world and their experiences; to think, and to feel; the faculty of consciousness and thought.

The mind is a thing of beauty. It contains all of our thoughts, reflections, ideas, values, beliefs and even feelings. Yes, indeed, also feelings. You cannot make up your mind without feelings!

If two options are rationally equal then, without feeling, you will not be able to decide. So, within the mind, logic and emotion are integrated. They are one and indivisible. When the mind grows, people grow. The quality of being, acting, thinking and feeling improves. When people grow, companies and communities grow. Becoming aware of how your and other minds are working and can grow, is one crucial step towards becoming a great person and leader. The one does not happen without the other.

The main challenge in this is to acknowledge and to overcome human instincts. Our brain is wired to protect ourselves and loved ones; to judge in an instant; to hold on to what we have; to read the minds of others instead of asking for information; to let emotions prevail; to regress to flight, fight or freeze behaviours when threatened; to show confidence before reason. And all of this is great, it is what makes us human, and it got us to where we are now. However, being aware of these instincts, and leading them in a way that's beneficial to ourselves and others, distinguishes us from other animals. So, for me, 'mind growing' is exactly that: acknowledging human instincts but learning how to master them in order to develop a mind that is open, respectful, curious and creative. It might sound naive, but I strongly feel it will lead us to a better, happier world.

In this book, I want to share insights and tools to grow and enrich the minds of people and, thus, of the collective mind of companies.

Marc Vanschoenwinkel
January 2020

ABOUT THE AUTHOR

Marc is a multilingual leadership and organizational development specialist with 30 years of experience in helping leaders around the globe to solve professional challenges.

With a Master's Degree in Clinical Psychology, Marc has a profound interest in the human psyche.

He has a passion for the dynamic interplay between personal growth and leadership styles. Throughout his long career, this fascination has driven him to push leaders on their own powerfully human paths of evolution and progress.

Growing up in a blue-collar family, Marc listened carefully while his parents shared stories about the trials of the everyday worker. Those kitchen table conversations deeply informed his attitudes on building an emotionally healthy workplace. Enlightened leadership, with the well-being of its workers as a goal, is fundamental to the future success of businesses, both large and small.

It is Marc's goal to help people shape a happy, productive workplace, with a focus on well-being, personal excellence, and growth.

Download your personal development logbook and watch demonstration videos on the book's website www.mindgrowing.net

PART I

Introduction

In Part I, I will describe the inspiration for and philosophy behind the concept of 'mind growing.' I will summarize the tool I have developed to achieve this, the New Leadership ABCs.

CHAPTER ONE

Mind Growing, Avoiding the 'Monkey Trap' and Embracing the Power of True Leadership

My core inspiration for writing this book is my belief that true leadership makes an enormous difference in the professional and private lives of so many people. I believe there is still enormous potential waiting to be developed within contemporary organisations. I wrote this book for every leader, or aspiring leader, who wants to develop their leadership abilities within what really is an exciting art and profession. Indeed, leadership should be seen as a profession equal to the technical knowledge and expertise every employee has.

I have over 30 years of experience as a consultant, coach, and trainer in leadership assessment and development. In my time in the field I have so often seen the influence that effective and true leadership can have on the happiness of people as well as on business results. Although there are many leaders who are good, willing and who have integrity, my heart is often bleeding out of compassion for the many leaders who are struggling, and their employees who bear the brunt. In modern enterprises, too many people seem to be prisoners of three core problems. Overcontrol or micromanagement, negative interaction patterns, and their own ego. These elements are closely interrelated, in the sense that one triggers the other, and together they often lead to a vicious cycle of demotivating interaction. Let's explore these three elements in more detail.

1. **Micromanagement.** The pressure put on leaders in contemporary companies is high. More and more, short-term numbers are defining the success or failure of organisations. Moreover, this is all happening within a global market that is rapidly changing and hard to keep a handle on. This puts a lot of pressure on the shoulders of those leading the company, and often this pressure is pushed down through the organisation to other leaders and employees. The first reaction to this challenging situation is so often to focus on control and efficiency. Because quick results are so important, it seems crucial that no mistakes are made. It is here that trust in people seems to get lost or, perhaps, for a lot of leaders, it's too dangerous to trust employees because too much is at stake. Thus, their solution is standardising and controlling as much as possible.

2. **Negative interaction patterns**. The effect on employees of micromanagement is of course that they feel controlled (and they are!), and the underlying message to them is, "We don't trust you." When people feel controlled, they become passive—they wait until someone says that they have to do something—and this lack of trust destroys their well-being, energy, and passion. And so, they end up being the opposite of what a leader is aiming for: they are not the trusted, energetic, and passionate people that will help realise the results that are so important.

3. **Ego.** These negative interaction patterns then reinforce the perception and convictions that already exist. Leaders then get trapped in their own belief system—their egos—and therefore lose track of other ways to shape interaction with employees. As a consequence, they feel that more control, pressure, and 'carrot and stick' type rewards have to be implemented. Of course, the effect on employees is...brutal!

But employees also often fuel this vicious cycle. They don't always see or feel the pressures that leaders are experiencing and the reasons behind their behaviour. This is probably because most of them are not directly in contact with the market or the shareholders. They don't necessarily have access to the bigger picture. Just like leaders, they are also often trapped in their own belief systems— their egos. They build up a defence system within themselves where they believe their leaders are stupid, do not know where they are going and what they are doing, or that they are only doing things to advance their own careers, and therefore they do not trust them. As I said before, it is difficult to see what came first: the attitude of the employees, the style of leadership, or the emphasis on short-term results. Ultimately, who is to blame is not that important. The important thing is making changes to get out of this rut. We often say that, as a leader, you are not always responsible for the current situation, as it can be inherited, but that you are always responsible for doing something about it, in order to shape the future. Of course, there is also a huge responsibility for shareholders and employees.

I often call this vicious cycle the 'monkey trap'. This is because, in these kinds of circumstances, humans revert to rather simple instinctive behaviour, because our limbic systems take a defensive mode. For the limbic system, social survival is crucial, and when trust is gone between colleagues it has to become defensive or even offensive to defend its own position. All kinds of basic emotions become stronger and more dominant. For example, feelings like, "I'm not respected," "Things are not fair," "Who is going to be the alpha?", "What is my position and how can I defend or improve it?", "The other person is the problem," and so on. And, again, it's cyclical, as this primal behaviour is demolishing whatever trust there is left.

The real challenge is not to lead the daily business: it is to 'grow our own mind,' and that of others, towards the realisation of our gigantic human potential. To do this, it is important to surpass our own egos, and those of others, to create real safety and freedom where people can be themselves. It means ridding ourselves of the basic human tendencies as described in the 'monkey trap.' The way forward is to become aware of these mechanisms that lead to destructive interaction and to become a lot more conscious about the way people, teams, and interactions function. This asks the following of leaders: vulnerability, authenticity, active listening, an open mind, and willingness to co-create. On the other hand, it is also important for leaders to give clear direction and a structured playing field, as there is no freedom without clear boundaries. If people don't know the direction of travel and where the boundaries are, it is very difficult to deploy their own initiative because the risk is too great if they do something wrong. They will be punished and, as a consequence, will undermine their own position.

To a great extent this is all related to the roles different parts of our brain play and how they interact with each other. If the emotional brain feels unsafe because of a lack of clarity or disrespect, the rational brain will be overtaken. In that moment your rational brain will no longer be heard and you will experience an instinctual stress reaction to danger - fight, flight, or freeze. Developing an awareness of this will give leaders the opportunity to change their style, to liberate the minds of people, and unleash the energy they already have in them to shape thriving companies. For this purpose, I offer a simple tool in this book, called the New Leadership ABCs. It gives you a framework for shaping a leadership style that liberates people from instinctive reactions. This allows them to 'grow' their own minds to become emotionally and intellectually stronger and independent. You can achieve this by focusing on:

A: Ambition
B: Boundaries
C: Culture and Coaching

The Need for New Paradigms in a Time of Change

Change is currently a hot topic in many organisations and the New Leadership ABCs provide a tool to support it. Many, if not all, organisations feel pressure from the rapidly changing world and don't want to be left behind. The changes I refer to are major change processes like substantial reorganisations and/or the transformation of culture. I often feel that a fundamental problem for most companies is that they are still based on a template that originated in the 19th century and developed a little bit in the 20th century. Although many trends and insights have led to changes over the years, the basic template for most organisations still seems to be based on Taylorism. Scientific management, also known as Taylorism after its founder Frederick Winslow Taylor, is a theory of management that analyses and synthesises workflows. The paradigm underlying this template is the belief that organisations, and the people working in them, are predictable, like machines. According to this theory, once you develop an effective machine, it is only a matter of pushing the right buttons for all to go as desired. Everything is foreseeable and can be planned. The idea that people are as predictable as machines began to change with the famous Hawthorne experiments in the 1920s and 1930s. Although they were testing the effect of working conditions on productivity (i.e. providing more light, some music ...), they discovered that it was not the change of conditions that increased production but the simple fact that they gave attention and respect to people by making them part of a scientific experiment. So, it was not the mechanical changes that played a major role but the emotional element of being seen as important. This is known as the Hawthorne Effect and it gave rise to the view that people are more than working machines; they are human beings who need to be given attention in order to develop.

I believe that employees are, first and foremost, human beings. They should be partners in your organisation and not just a means of production. However, in many respects these old views have not fundamentally changed; employees are still viewed as predictable machines that need attention, training and, once in a while, a 'carrot' or a 'hit with a stick.' Daniel Pink made a strong case when he stated that the 'carrot and stick' approach is only effective for repetitive mechanical tasks. Whenever a task demands thinking, the 'carrot and stick' approach loses its power and more intrinsic motivation is needed. As Pink suggests, people are intrinsically motivated when they work within an environment that gives them purpose, autonomy and mastery.

These old paradigms worked seemingly fine when the environment was relatively stable and predictable, as it was for most of the last two centuries. But, in our current environment, we need a paradigm shift acknowledging that the world is not mechanical, but instead organic. People are sense-making, purpose-driven, and creative beings, motivated by their feelings and interpretations of the world. A fixed mechanical structure can no longer survive in our organic and changing world. We need more loosely assembled networks that reflect this new context and allow for:

- a high level of autonomy (for people and groups of people).

- acting on the basis of the same organisational DNA (a shared purpose, values and boundaries).

- connection by emotional gravity (an emotional connection with the network, its people, its purpose and its values).

These kinds of networks can be organic, as they have a high adaptability to changing circumstances. But, being realistic, I know that most organisations don't have the desire to change that much. What I do foresee are a great number of them looking to move away from Taylorism and finding a more flexible and agile way of working. For this, 'mind growing' and the New Leadership ABCs are an effective tool.

A company and its employees blocked by perceptions and emotions not tackled by leadership

A few years ago, I was part of a team facilitating a cultural change process for a large IT company. For many years they had been insourcing IT activities, services, and even whole departments from other companies. The leaders never spent much effort integrating all these different groups and little attention was given to communication, connections, or people's feelings and perceptions. Employee engagement surveys showed deep demotivation and disconnection from the company, and results were going down as a consequence. Management saw the lack of motivation as a more or less unavoidable phenomenon in times of high pressure. The company was keeping its head above water by reinforcing quality through an enormous amount of control.

When we were facilitating the cultural transformation process it became clear that, because of this lack of interest in them as human beings, the employees had little to no trust in their managers. Managers no longer trusted employees either because of the lack of results. With large-scale interventions including dialogue sessions between all parties (with a lot of listening and exploring of each other's perspectives), leadership training, and co-creation of a new way forward, perceptions on both sides were corrected and trust was rebuilt. In retrospect, it took a huge amount of energy to fix something that never should have been broken.

Unwilling people make working systems fail and willing people make unworking systems work.

Filip Vandendriessche

CHAPTER TWO

The New Leadership ABCs in a Nutshell: A Tool for Growth

What are the New Leadership ABCs?

The New Leadership ABCs will help to free and 'grow' the minds of people with great results for your company. It is an easy-to-use structure for creating a leadership style that will reframe instinctive human reactions. This, in turn, will create space for authentic personal growth, passion and engagement. It is also aimed at shaping an environment where independent but loyal and attached employees will be able to react in a flexible way to changing circumstances. This is what organisations currently need in our rapidly changing environment. But perhaps more important is that the New Leadership ABCs are based on recent insights from brain research. It is a leadership approach that nourishes the needs of different parts of the brain, for both leaders and employees.

It gives employees a clear direction and playing field that offers meaning, safety, and predictability. Within that playing field they are given space for autonomy and mastery. It is influenced by the SCARF model of behaviour, developed by David Rock, and it explains how best to manage people and collaborate at work from a brain-science perspective. SCARF defines the different social elements that, when not respected, light up parts of our brain that indicate real physical pain. These elements are: lack of status; lack of certainty about the future; no (or very limited) autonomy; a lack of relatedness to a group; and the absence of fairness. I will explain them in further detail in Chapter Four, which discusses neuroleadership and personality development.

But for leaders, essentially, the proposed New Leadership ABCs style respects the SCARF elements. This is because the essence of the model is to stay "in the lead," but on a different level. Instead of being too much on an operational level, with a lot of instructions, micromanagement and control, in the New Leadership ABCs the role and the power of the leader is in defining and safeguarding a direction, ambition and a clear playing field. In that way, the leader keeps their predictability—as far as this is still possible in our current world—autonomy, and relatedness.

In order to achieve this, the main changes leadership has to make (for the benefit of leaders, employees and organisations) is moving;

from being too much in control and in the mode of selling solutions (which are often new processes and standardisation—so again, more control)

to letting go of the urge to micromanage and focussing on defining a core ambition, a large enough playing field, and making sure that there is the necessary coaching and culture where people can act and create. In this way, people will be able to find the way (i.e. the solutions) to achieve the ambition themselves.

In sum, instead of managing too much on a very concrete operational level, there are three elements which allow you to manage on a higher level and still keep control of and responsibility for the end results. These three elements are:

A: Ambition
B: Boundaries
C: Culture and Coaching

Ambition, Boundaries and Coaching

So, here you have the New Leadership ABCs:

Ambition
It is important to formulate an ambition that comes from the heart and which is authentic. I will describe where core ambition comes from and how you can find it.

This is about formulating the goals that make it worth getting out of bed each morning. For example, "We want to create products and services that give people more time to spend with their loved ones."

Make sure that you engage people on this level. They must feel and share the importance of this ambition. And, while I may have created the impression that it needs to be your ambition, this is not necessarily the case, and perhaps it is better if it isn't. The important thing is that the ambition has to be supported and carried, in the first instance, by you as a leader. But it can be developed by the participation and input of employees, to different degrees, from no input to a lot of co-creation. In fact, I think it's necessary and wise to stimulate input and co-creation from different parties (internally and externally) in order to define the ambition. When people are involved, they will support an idea in an engaged and motivated way. However, I feel that, as a leader, you can only champion an ambition if it connects with your own heart and beliefs, and it is always you who must integrate, summarise and state the final aims and direction.

Boundaries

When I talk about boundaries, I am not talking about a manual full of rules. I am talking about a few core values that form the boundaries for which behaviours and solutions are desired and acceptable within the company you want to lead. This is the playing field. Make sure that they are crystal clear, and that you follow them yourself. Whenever possible, be open about boundaries employees have to respect. Without boundaries, the world becomes an unsafe place for most people; instead of taking initiative, they will remain passive to avoid making mistakes. In that sense, boundaries have the special quality of being both limiting and freeing at the same time.

For example, if employees have a €5,000 budget to find a solution for a problem, then they are limited to the €5,000, but they also have the freedom of having the €5,000 at their disposal. Where they might second-guess themselves and spend very little if they don't know what they are 'allowed' to spend, they are now able to find the best resources for the job without fear of upsetting management.

Ambition + Boundaries = The DNA of your leadership and the company you are shaping

I see the combination of ambition and boundaries as so fundamental that I consider them the DNA of leadership. After all, if you radiate a clear ambition, straight from the heart, and create a playing field in which the boundaries are made up of your own key values, the fundamentals of your leadership are already there. When these form the core of your communication, and when expressed as purpose (ambition) and possibilities (the positive side of boundaries), they will have such a strong influence that they will start to lead and shape all actions and interactions within your team, department, or organisation. They form a code and whatever an employee of your company does has to be in accordance with and shaped by this code.

And, of course, the more influence you have within your team, department, or company, the more your ambition and boundaries will define its DNA.

Culture and Coaching

Perhaps, by now, I have instilled the idea that if you formulate an ambition and a playing field that your job as a leader is finished. But nothing could be further from the truth! The whole purpose of the New Leadership ABCs is that you take things to a higher level, by defining ambition and the playing field, and that by doing so you create an inspiring space for people to take initiative, find their own solutions and develop new ideas. So, in this way, you make your employees responsible.

However, you would be leading an ideal team or organisation if each and every employee was willing and able to carry out their responsibilities on their own initiative. I think it is often the opposite. In a lot of companies, people are taught and strongly encouraged to follow instructions and manuals. And, as explained earlier, this tends to break down the intrinsic motivation in people. However, when you restore their autonomy, motivation won't always return immediately. People are not often very logical beings. Although science says that they will be intrinsically motivated when they get purpose, autonomy, and mastery—as the author Daniel Pink describes in his book, Drive: The Surprising Truth About What Motivates Us—the first reaction when they are given more freedom and space is fear and passivity. This is because people easily get stuck in patterns. If they were conditioned, in the past, to follow detailed guidelines and instructions, they will be afraid to take more of their own initiative. They will fear making mistakes and being punished. So, if you as a leader leave it to them to define ambition and boundaries, then a lot of them will withdraw and show no initiative whatsoever. That's why you have to guide and coach them.

This means that you have to check if people are:

1. **Aware** of what is expected from them, and how important it is to take their own initiative.

2. **Willing** to do as expected (e.g. What are the hurdles they see and how can they be tackled?)

3. **Able** to do as expected (e.g. Do they have the right knowledge and skills?)

4. **Courageous** enough to change their behaviour (e.g. Offer them safety and safety nets to encourage change).

These four elements need to be regularly checked (and coached) so it's possible for employees to act with initiative and ownership, within the framework defined by the ambition and the playing field. How to tackle these four elements and the skills needed for coaching, will be further elaborated on in Chapter Eight.

Applying the New Leadership ABCs Will Build Emotional Gravity

By being consistent with your ambition and inspiration, by making the playing field explicit and clear on an ongoing basis, and by coaching people to develop their awareness, willingness, mastery and courage you will create a strong alignment and attachment between employees and your company. Their brains and hearts will be nourished. That is why we call this 'building emotional gravity'; people will be emotionally connected to your company—a force much bigger than formal labour contracts and all kinds of financial bonuses.

In later chapters, I will describe tips, tools, and strategies that will help you to apply the New Leadership ABCs. Here, I give you the first of many real-world examples of implementation that will give you an insight into how the model works in practice.

A transformation process, respecting our brains

The strongest transformation I ever co-facilitated was for a company that wanted to boost their customer experience. They decided that creating awareness was the most important aspect for success, which took us nearly a year to implement. Imagine eight months in which people could chew on the ambition, and reflect and co-construct ideas within the given boundaries. We tapped into the energy of people by organising open space sessions where about 100 employees could together define an agenda and discuss different topics related to what they saw as being important to exceed customers' expectations. They also had workshops and training to acquire the necessary skills and to discuss how customer expectations could be exceeded. Taskforces took topics coming from these events and used them to develop specific solutions.

In a way, it was a very organic process and the content was not as important as the interaction, energy, and reflection that was created. But all of this work led to the desired results. The ambition was clear as well as the boundaries and the playing field. Moments were created where energy was unleashed for people to co-create solutions. The workshops and training sessions served to coach people during this organic process.

Leadership is "giving" problems and "receiving solutions", not the other way around.

Filip Vandendriessche

PART II

The Origins of Mind Growing and the New Leadership ABCs

In this section and the next, I will elaborate on the context that originated 'mind growing' and the New Leadership ABCs. This context is twofold:

1. The rapidly changing world, its consequences for how organisations are organised and operated, and the need for a paradigm shift. This I will explore within Chapter Three.

2. The extensive knowledge we have gathered during the last decade in neuroscience. This has taught us a tremendous amount about how the brain functions, shedding light on how to lead and motivate people. I will elaborate this in Chapter Four on neuroleadership and personality development.

The Rapidly Changing World and the Need for a Paradigm Shift

The world in which we live and work is rapidly changing. The Internet forms a structure that greatly resembles the human nervous system. It connects everyone. Information is instantly available, with just one click. This means that consumers often know more about the products they are buying than the salesperson. They become more and more critical, and expect tailor-made products and services instead of standardised ones. A simple idea can propel a company to success in just a few years. And, in the blink of an eye, you can have a new and very successful competitor. In this world, where things change so quickly, one can rely less and less on fixed structures, standardisation and control.

Quick adaptability and innovation become increasingly important. Therefore, you need well-trained and motivated employees who can take their own initiative within a clear framework. The framework, constituted by the ambition and the playing field, will provide good direction for motivated employees. Teams can use this to orient themselves to undertake appropriate action. However, this means that the company's ambitions and values must be strongly held in the hearts and minds of each employee. This will help to create a company that can be flexible, where people have energy, are open to hearing new ideas, and where these new ideas can flow. Doesn't this seem logical?

In the 19th and 20th centuries, when industries arose, the main challenges were to efficiently produce as much as possible, to sell goods and services to the masses, and to make a good profit.

Delivering a consistent quality over time, and to different customers, became an important challenge. It was not acceptable that the quality of your car depended on the variable quality of work by people in the factory who made it.

All of these challenges ask for a high level of management, in the form of standardised working methods, clear procedures, control of activities, quality and regulation. And all of this is still important; we still want to guarantee good quality products and services for everyone, and we still want to work in efficient and effective ways. There is nothing wrong with that. However, as markets evolve, and a demand develops for tailor-made and personalised products and services, this becomes more difficult to prioritise. To a certain extent, this is still theoretically possible within the paradigm of old school management (structure, control, standardisation), but, in our current context, this model seems to have reached its limit. People have access to plenty of information and possibilities; they are connected to each other worldwide; new business ideas pop up quite easily; people can shop internationally and have more choices than ever. This is why we need a paradigm shift from a mostly management to a mostly leadership perspective.

Here again, is where the New Leadership ABCs finds its place and its challenge to solve. Management is about doing things effectively, efficiently, and in a standardised way. Leadership is about finding the right direction, inspiring and developing people, and creating teams and employees that can take their own actions in flexible but consistent ways. Leaders let things flow, like water down a river, putting the right stones in the riverbed to make sure that the water flows in the right direction. And, although a lot of companies try to develop leaders in this way, the success ratio does not seem to be very high. It seems to me that the main reason for this is that companies don't make this fundamental paradigm shift.

Gerry Johnson and Kevan Scholes, when explaining their concept of the Cultural Web, state that often the first reaction of management to the lack of success of their company is to improve efficiency and effectiveness—in other words, cost reduction. When this is tried a few times with little success, the next step they often take is to revise the strategy of the company, which is also not the solution. This is because a new strategy is often the same strategy, sold differently. What companies seldom do is to rethink their fundamental paradigm or culture. By this, I mean their key beliefs about their reason for existence i.e. what the market needs, what leadership should look like, and how the company should work. Current times and context are asking for a paradigm shift on all of these elements, as well as how we think about leadership. Exploring the core paradigm at the centre of your company can be done using the Cultural Web tool. I will go into more detail in Chapter Eight on culture and coaching.

I describe one of the strongest paradigm shifts I experienced within my career in the next case.

How a famous retailer adapted to changing times

I've done a lot of work over the last few decades for a large retail company. Because of our long-term relationship, I could experience and participate in the need for transformation that was forced on them around the end of the 1990s and the beginning of the 2000s. For decades they were very successful by always implementing the same standardised concept in almost every country in the world. This was smart, as the concept was well elaborated and well thought of. It was developed by the best, and perfected over several decades. Time after time it proved how well it worked. But then the world began to change, quickly and drastically.

One of the major factors was the Internet and the possibilities it offered for online shopping. Customers suddenly began to expect more variety, more personal and custom-made services, and easier access wherever they were. My client, who was attached for many decades to their approach, had to change drastically, and they are still in the process of changing at the moment of writing this book. They are exploring more and very different formulas, online and offline, to create a great customer experience, and are aligning services to the needs of their customers in different countries. This required completely different skills for their employees as well as their leaders, which eventually led to a new company culture. Leadership needed to foster more agility, customer focus, and the need for more exploration—finding new ideas in almost every field. A change in the market has led to an exciting journey for this company, and also for me, for which I will be forever grateful.

We can't solve problems by using the same kind of thinking we used when we created them.

Albert Einstein

CHAPTER FOUR

Neuroleadership and Personality Development

In this chapter, I describe the role different parts of the brain play in creating personality and behaviour. I also show the relevance of the brain in leadership and change.

Never before has there been so much research and knowledge available concerning how the brain works. The brain started to fascinate me 30 years ago when my professor at the time, Jean-Pierre De Waele, said, "The brain is the only organ that studies itself." How exciting is that?

But, first let me describe the different evolutionary parts of the brain. I will limit myself to a simplified description of the different elements and their impacts on communication, leadership, and personality development.

The 'Crocodile Brain'

Figure 4.1 The brainstem, highlighted in red

About 500 million years ago, a being similar to a crocodile crawled out of the ocean. This animal's brain was what we call the brainstem, more popularly referred to as the reptile or crocodile brain (I will use the term crocodile brain from this point onwards). The function of this brain was, and still is (because it is still a part of our brain), sheer survival. Nothing less, nothing more. One crucial task of the crocodile brain is to filter the approximately 10,000 stimuli we receive per second. Most of these stimuli are completely irrelevant and will never come into the conscious mind. However, when a stimulus is relevant for survival, the crocodile brain springs into action. When threatened, our responses are very limited. They are either fight, flight, or freeze. In other words, mate and eat when the opportunity is there, because at any time a predator might injure or kill you.

When you, as a leader, raise your voice, shout, or throw things (oh yes, it happens), or when you become too demanding, you will threaten their crocodile brain. It will put people into fight, flight or freeze mode, and you will no longer be able to deliver anything useful to the situation.

The Limbic Brain

Figure 4.2 The limbic brain, highlighted in orange

The next part to develop was the limbic brain, about 300 million years ago, (so about 200 million years after the development of the crocodile brain). The limbic brain is also called the mammal brain. There are many differences between reptiles and mammals, but the biggest one is probably that most mammals live in groups, like our first ancestors about four million years ago. Living in a group is a major and effective strategy to increase your chance of survival. However, in order to live in a group, certain behaviour is needed to make it possible for both the individual and the group to survive. The limbic brain makes this possible. For example, one part of the limbic brain regulates position and hierarchy within a group. Living in a group creates some contradictory dynamics, which have to be resolved. Some individuals within groups have strong positions within the hierarchy, which gives them more opportunities to feed and mate. However, if every member becomes strong, dominant, and is only concerned with their own interests, the group will disintegrate because of fighting. In this way, the limbic brain regulates things so that individuals can sense when other individuals are more dominant or submissive, and where there are opportunities to improve one's own position within the group. It also allows for estimating whether other individuals are friendly (taking into account the interests of others), or threatening (motivated only by their own satisfaction and survival). Keep this idea in mind for later in the book, as these are still the two main dimensions that have a big influence on interactions between people.

Thus, the main function of the limbic system is (social) sensing and feeling, in order to create the strongest position possible for the individual, while also keeping the group stable enough to survive the threatening external world. To reconcile these two different interests— the individual and the group—the limbic brain is able to read small, non-verbal signals that give information about when to prioritise one's own interests and when to back down in the interests of the group. One very important characteristic of the limbic brain is the fact that it has a memory for emotions in combination with situations. It remembers when a situation is pleasant, frustrating, and certainly when it is threatening. And, of course, it remembers situations in terms of general or striking characteristics.

When we were building our house in Spain, our Jack Russell Terrier stole the lunch of one of the builders, and he was yelled at in Spanish. Now, every time we have Spanish people over to the house, he stays far away from them. It seems that his limbic brain made the connection between the sound of the Spanish language and a negative emotion; his limbic brain took control and selected flight as a reaction. Humans still have this brain and the same sort of thing happens to us. If, for example, you received a lot of negative feedback from your mother when you were younger, the limbic brain probably associates female authority figures with a negative feeling. Years later, when you have a female manager for the first time, your limbic brain may cause you to have a fight, flight or freeze reaction, often without you knowing that the origin of these tendencies has nothing to do with your manager, but is instead based on the relationship with your mother.

The limbic system can also (unconsciously) remember the link between a previous situation, its emotions, and an effective way to respond. In the example of your mother, the recurrent negative feedback gives you a bad feeling and you react with a 'moving away' response. Perhaps your 'moving away' response is fighting, and your brain notices that this works. You learn, on an emotional level, that by arguing about why you did something, you see or feel that she changes her mind, and the negative feelings you experience change into neutral or even positive feelings. What the limbic system remembers and will use in the future, is that a female authority figure equals a bad feeling, and you have to defend yourself because this is the most effective response. You can imagine that in social situations this can start a vicious cycle. Your limbic brain will start in a defensive mode, possibly triggering offensive behaviour against your female leader. Because you argue defensively about why something is wrong in a certain situation (which may be perceived as excuses), your female manager will do her best to give you feedback about your own behaviour, because she wants to make you conscious about your role in getting things right. So, in a sense, you push her into a role like that of your mother!

All parts of the brain like predictability, as does the limbic brain. The whole of our brain is a kind of error-detecting machine based on our conscious (rational) and unconscious (limbic) expectations. So, if you encounter a female leader who doesn't fit your unconscious associations of a female giving you negative feedback, your limbic system really becomes concerned. The reaction is often to deform reality by selective perception, so that the world becomes predictable again. Or, if deforming is not possible, then often an even stronger reaction will occur, in the form of fight, flight, or freeze. She might give you nothing but compliments, but if she gives you one negative piece of feedback it will be the latter you will remember. All of this happens unconsciously. You may have no idea what is happening and why your relationships with female leaders are often so difficult. This can, of course, also work in a positive way. Suppose that your mother was warm, supportive, and encouraging. In that case, the limbic brain will remember that a female authority figure equals very positive associations. You will probably enjoy and look for female leaders, perhaps not even seeing their flaws or the instances where they are not encouraging and supportive.

Does this mean that we are all driven by unconscious drives based on limbic superiority (supported by the crocodile brain), and that there is no conscious free will? To a certain extent it is exactly what this means. But there is still the last brain to discuss, the neo-cortex.

The Neo-cortex

This is our rational supervisor, and there is a mutual influence between this rational part and the more automatic (crocodile) and emotional (limbic) parts. Science shows that behaviour is initiated in the limbic brain. So, during an argument, it is possible that your hand is already making a fist without you consciously being aware of it, and even without you rationally wanting to hit somebody. The impulse to hit someone, originated by the limbic brain, then passes through the rational brain for one tenth of a second. Imagine that free will is only one tenth of a second. It is the time in which you can rationally decide to continue or to abort the physical action started.

One could say that the relationship between the different parts of the brain is quite complex. They help each other and they fight with each other at the same time. Just like in a real team, they each have their own role and place, but sometimes they all want to be in control. The three brains put together help you to survive physically (crocodile), socially (the limbic system), and allow you to shape your environment and plan your future (rational neo-cortex). But there is no use in shaping and planning if you don't survive. That is why the crocodile and the limbic brain are able to take over when your physical (crocodile) and social (limbic) survival is in danger. In both cases they don't hesitate to take control with their rather rudimentary reactions of fight, flight or freeze. This is like shooting a cannon at a mosquito. It is drastic though effective, in the sense that the mosquito will probably be dead as well as everything around it. But this kind of response is not very effective in our current and complex reality where it's necessary to kill only the mosquito.

The Ambitions of the Limbic Brain

Both systems, the crocodile and limbic brain, also have a positive drive and, with some imagination, you could call this ambition. But don't expect too much from the crocodile brain, as its sole ambition is to eat and mate as much as possible, or at least when it is necessary. For the limbic brain, the ambition is social and emotional: the drive to be part of a group (better chance of survival); to have an emotional and social bond with group members (to avoid being kicked out); and to have a good position within the group (more opportunity to eat and to mate). This is why emotional, social, and physical contact is so important to the limbic brain. Having those things soothes the limbic brain. Not having those things, or if they are being threatened, makes the limbic brain active and it will take control.

The limbic brain is also wary of social threat (losing position and being excluded from the group). One way in which it aims to keep position and belonging within a group is the development of an emotional memory, where it connects all kinds of social and group situations to an emotion. In this way, it builds a reserve of experiences that it can use to handle various situations that can occur when living in a group i.e. dealing, competing, and collaborating with other individuals. Many of these connections are built in early life, when the limbic system is in control (the neo-cortex still has to develop after birth), but they can be constructed at almost any age when you encounter situations with a high emotional impact.

Influencing the Limbic Brain through Leadership

Let's go back to this idea of a social threat that came into existence with the appearance of the limbic brain. This is crucial for contemporary organisations as the limbic brain is very influential and initiates behaviour. One could say that all behaviour that is shown or wanted is initiated in the limbic brain. Also, its influence on the rational brain is just as strong, perhaps stronger than the neo-cortex's influence on the limbic brain, depending on the individual, as it often becomes absolute when physical or social integrity is in danger. You will be limited, as a leader, without having an impact on the limbic brain of the people you influence. On the other hand, when you, as a person, and certainly as a leader, threaten the physical (and we presume that this is rarely the case in our modern times), or the social integrity (which we unfortunately see happen very often in contemporary organisations), your influence will be zero. It may even have a negative impact, because people will start to boycott you, often in an invisible way. So, how can you have an influence on the limbic brain?

Let's get some inspiration from our distant family members, the chimpanzees. For them, the crocodile and the limbic brain are the most important. When working in Australia, I had the honour of meeting Andrew O'Keeffe, author of Hardwired Humans, the fascinating book about our human instincts and their consequences for current organisations and leadership. During a presentation of his that I attended, he talked about his observations of male chimpanzees in Australian zoos as well as Jane Goodall's observations in the jungle about the way chimpanzees became the alpha male of the group.

He first talked about Frodo, who was a bully from childhood. His peers stopped playing with him and started to flee when he arrived. But, through dominance and bullying, he became the alpha male. With the limbic brain sensitive to hierarchal position, it is possible to dominate and become the alpha by inducing fear. For others it is a sheer matter of survival to be submissive to this kind of dominance. But Frodo had a small problem. The first opportunity the group saw to get rid of him, by supporting younger potential alpha males, they did. Frodo's career was rather limited in time; he was alpha for only two years.

He made some attempts to reach the alpha position again, but here sources differ in their information. Some say that he succeeded a few times, but never for a long period. Other sources say that he failed and became a shadow of his former self.

Another way to have an impact on the limbic brain was shown by Figen. He almost never acted aggressively when it wasn't necessary. Most of the time he was just sitting and looking wisely at his group, giving them all the freedom possible to do their own things. Only when some of them didn't behave or didn't follow the rules of the group did he intervene to correct them in a firm way. I think that Figen, in all his chimp wisdom, found one of the golden rules of effective leadership: set the boundaries and the culture, act immediately when these are not respected, but give freedom wherever possible.

Lubutu showed a similar but subtly different style of leadership. Unusual for an alpha male in a chimp community, he was very friendly to females and their offspring. One time he had to go to the veterinarian for about half a day. In the evening, when he came back, another alpha male had taken the leadership position. But what happened over the course of that night was extraordinary. All the females started to return to Lubutu, turning their backs on the new leader. In the morning, Lubutu was back in his alpha position.

Another leadership style was seen in Mike. He found some plastic cans and bashed them together to make all the noise he could, clapping himself to the alpha position. The group was so impressed with his performance that they accepted his leadership. This style, I suppose, rings a bell when looking at certain current organisations.

What can we learn from these examples about the ways a leader can have an impact on the limbic brains of their people?

Of course, there is dominance: if you are more aggressive, stronger and bigger than the others, their limbic brains will be submissive to protect themselves. This protection happens in two ways. Firstly, by being submissive to the stronger chimp, you keep yourself physically and socially safe. You don't get harmed and you will keep your position within the group. Challenging a strong alpha male could risk both. Secondly, by accepting the leadership of strong and aggressive alpha males, the limbic brain feels the group is protected from outside danger, and also from inside destabilisation. So, dominance and aggressiveness also have a clear function within a social group. I am convinced that a leader needs a certain amount of dominance and the ability to show his teeth when necessary. Jane Goodall reported instances where this was lacking with the leader, leading to an unstable and disintegrated group, with a lot of fear and infighting. However, if you are dominant and you only defend your own interests, then your leadership can be very limited. It can last only if you stay strong, don't get sick or hurt, or when there are no other strong alphas aiming to take your role.

Author Patrick Vermeren cites evidence that leaders in the first human communities were only leaders because of the communities themselves. When a leader became too dominant, unfair, or only protected his own interests, he was no longer supported and was removed from the leadership position. It was only when humans discovered agriculture, stayed in one place, and when ownership of land and stocks became a source of richness and power, that leaders started to defend and expand their position, detached from the support of the community.

Thus, there are two main strategies to obtain a stronger position within a group by having a strong impact on the limbic brain of others. They are 1) getting ahead, and 2) getting ahead by getting along. The dominance approach is part of the getting ahead strategy. One could say that Mike, with his plastic cans, was also using the getting ahead approach, not with the use of physical power but with the use of physical attributes. Both styles are based on showing off. In contrast, the getting ahead by getting along approach was used by Figen and Lubutu. They had impact on the limbic brain by inducing positive feelings; they gave others in the group freedom, respect, and disciplined chimps not respecting the rules of effective social cohabitation. And the most striking thing is that they got further ahead by getting along.

The SCARF Model

David Rock made the most striking and complete description of how we can have a positive or negative impact on the limbic brain with his SCARF model. In his 2008 paper, "SCARF: A Brain-Based Model for Collaborating with and Influencing Others," Rock describes brain research that shows that not respecting the SCARF elements activates the same brain areas as inflicting physical pain. People will stop listening and they will go into fight, flight, or freeze mode. But the inverse is also true, and this is very interesting. Interacting with people in such a way that you respect the SCARF elements will trigger intrinsic motivation and a response to you as a leader. People will be motivated to follow you without the need for control. Always keep in mind that it is impossible to be a leader without people willing to follow you.

Here is my description of the different SCARF elements and how they relate to the previous information about the limbic brain:

Status

Although formal status is certainly a part of this, it is even more about the fact that I need a place and role in the group which is respected and valued. Even when I am in the lowest position, perhaps not the ideal one, at least I have a place and role in the group, and it is secure. When I have a higher status within the group, it comes with more opportunities for mating, eating, survival, and thus transmitting my gene pool to the next generation. So, position or status within a group is, for the limbic brain, crucial for survival. People and animals accept differences in status and, to a certain extent, it can be functional as it shows clearly who has power and influence. However, if the differences in status become too big then it causes stress and dissatisfaction. The acceptance of differences in status are also culturally determined. Geert Hofstede's six dimensions of national cultures theory shows us that a distance between positions, whereby a higher position gets more privileges, is more acceptable in some cultures than in others, based on societal values. For example, in the Middle East, hierarchy and status are highly respected constructs that are intrinsic to the way they perceive the world. In the Netherlands and Scandinavian countries, it is often the opposite.

Changes in position, or a disrespect of my role and value, are experienced as life threatening. So, when you, as a leader, lower the status of someone, you can expect a strong reaction in the form of fight, flight, or freeze. There is also a continuous natural drive to improve your position. This is where status (making your position externally visible) is crucial. Think of Mike with his plastic cans, which gave him status leading him to the alpha position.

Linking this all to leadership, the message is: handle status with care. Making denigrating remarks or jokes at someone else's expense, not taking someone seriously, taking away symbols of status (a title, car, an office with a window), giving some advice or feedback...all of this can be seen as undermining the status of a worker, leading to fight, flight or freeze behaviours. Whatever the reaction, it will expend a huge amount of energy and stress. On the other hand, treating people as mature adults, with fundamental respect for who they are and what they think, will give them an incredible boost to their feeling of status. In this sense, communication is crucial. So, make sure to listen to people, value their input, appreciate the positive things they do, deal with them as adults, be as transparent as possible, give them facts and numbers, and don't sugar-coat messages.

In Chapter Nine I explain the levels of communication. The core of this concept is the fact that when you are communicating (verbally and/or non-verbally), you are always communicating on different levels, of which the relationship level is the most important. With almost everything you say to someone, there is a (usually) hidden message about how you define the relationship with that person, and how you see their status in relation to yours (higher, lower or the same level). The core concepts from transactional analysis are also relevant here. This concept tells us that people can talk and act from three different positions called ego states: namely parent (with an important subdivision between caring and regulating parent), adult and child. So, when you are interacting with someone, you can be, without realising it, in the parent role with your co-worker in the child role. When interactions between different people take place, all kinds of combinations can occur— people will be in different states depending on who they are interacting with. However, it is good to know that when you, as a leader, communicate too much from either the caring or the regulating parent position, you tend to violate the status principle. The side effect will be that you push them into a child role where they might become playful, irresponsible and dependent. The same goes for employees who have a tendency to act from the child position. They will push you, as the leader, into the parent role. This often leads to a vicious pattern, which is not easy to break without external help.

Certainty
The brain, as a whole, is a pattern-recognizing and error-detecting machine. When something happens that is not according to expected patterns, then the brain detects an error. The brain is addicted to predictability. Without it, the world becomes unsafe as the pattern recognition is no longer effective and we can no longer anticipate and adapt our behaviour to survive—physically and socially. When an error occurs, and prediction is no longer possible, the brain will put all of its energy and attention into the error and not into normal things like work, attaining goals, or making plans. So, as a leader, it is useful to keep the world as predictable as possible. You can do this by describing the future; what can be expected; what outcomes will be; or which problems can be expected and how they can be solved. This will help people focus on shaping their world and the future, instead of thinking up all kinds of wild threats to detect and avoid.
My own experience tells me that the person—and the personality—is crucial in leadership. If you, as an employee, feel that you can trust your leader to keep you informed, help you, and protect you whenever they can, then this provides enough predictability and safety. When the world around you becomes increasingly unpredictable, and your leaders provide little stability or consistency, it's a very different story.

Autonomy

Autonomy gives us control. The brain is driven to detect errors and to initiate appropriate action when needed. The ability to act in this way is key to survival, but it requires a level of autonomy. If this is not possible, or limited to a great extent, you can imagine the threat it represents. It is like being locked in a box with deadly snakes and not being able to do anything. The levels of cortisol in your body will grow, creating stress, and the urge to fight or flee will increase. However, studies also show that cortisol doesn't keep rising forever. After a while it decreases and you get used to the situation.

As a leader, there are two possibilities. You can choose to withhold autonomy or give autonomy within clear criteria and boundaries:

1. Employees see the need to act but don't have the possibility to do so. The levels of cortisol will rise and will induce a huge amount of stress, often leading to burnout. Or, after a while, the stress reduces and people get used to and accept the situation. In that case they become passive and not driven to act or change things for the better. Frankly, we see this happening everywhere when people are micromanaged and/or over-controlled.

2. On the other hand, you can provide autonomy with caveats. As Daniel Pink tells us, extensive research shows that having autonomy is one of the key factors in creating intrinsic motivation. But you, as a leader, also want autonomy and control. That's why this book focuses so much attention on defining a playing field with clear boundaries. It means that you formulate the values and criteria within which they can act. It gives autonomy to employees and control to you as the leader. It is putting people in a meadow where in some corners there are perhaps some snakes to deal with. There are boundaries, but they have enough space to find an effective solution without having their hands tied. So, the main tip here is, avoid micromanagement. Don't try to find all the solutions yourself—you're a leader, not a specialist. Give people autonomy and train them so that they can handle it. Micromanagement is, in my opinion, only appropriate when dealing with strategically important details.

Relatedness

I suppose that the importance of relatedness needs little further explanation. The thread throughout this chapter about neuroleadership is the limbic brain's understanding that being part of a group is a crucial element of physical and social survival. SCARF's understanding of relatedness is focussed on whether I am in or out of the group. 'In' means safety—at least in relation to the threats from the outside world. 'Out' means being exposed to the numerous threats to physical existence and procreation. Relatedness means the possibility to have safe relationships. These are relationships in which the other can be trusted. The limbic brain decides in a split second if someone is a friend or an enemy. Here again is the importance of non-verbal communication: what is the message between the lines about how you see the relationship with the other person and their status compared to yours? For example, walking into a meeting without shaking hands and looking people in the eye for a second can convey the message that the people present are not important to you. It is not rare to see a leader take a forum for an hour to express how important people are for him, and how crucial it is to listen to each other, without having one moment of interaction with them, or allowing the audience to say or ask anything. It is what we call an incongruence between words (what you say) and actions. It is important to know that your actions are always overruling your words. What and how you act (non-verbal behaviour), is much more influential and convincing than what you say (verbal behaviour). Research says that 70 per cent of communication happens non-verbally and only 30 per cent is verbal. This also depends on culture and its connected values and norms. More about this when we discuss the neo-cortex.

In my experience, I have found that trust has a lot to do with being consistent and vulnerable. Vulnerability makes you human and shows that you are real. When you are real, people know that there are probably no hidden agendas or bad intentions. The more people can read your heart and mind—the more transparency you give—the more predictable and trusted you become. Being consistent goes beyond the famous expression of "walking the walk". Even stronger is to walk first and then talk. Show, as a leader, in your behaviour, what you want or desire from others and then start talking about it.

Fairness
There is hard evidence to state that the basis for morality is already present within the limbic brain. For me, this sounds logical, as it seems to be a core necessity for a group to function in an effective way. Living in a group means that you have to reconcile different interests. In that sense, it is no surprise that the limbic brain was wired to have a sense of fairness. I refer here to the work of Frans de Waal with capuchin monkeys. On YouTube you can find astonishing videos where he shows that they have a strong sense of fairness. Also, the work of Jan van Hoof (also on YouTube) is a wonderful demonstration of how fairness (also in the sense of making sure that different interests are served) is already present in primates. In these videos one can see that if monkeys perform exactly the same tasks, but get a different reward, the one who gets the perceived lesser reward

When you **violate** one of the following elements

Status

Certainty

Autonomy

Relatedness

Fairness

Emotional parts of the **brain** take over and steer behaviour towards

FIGHT

FLIGHT

FREEZE

Figure 4.3 The importance of the SCARF elements to the limbic brain

becomes very angry. The desire for equality is central to this sense of fairness. When that feeling of unfairness is present, it is received in the limbic brain as a threat.

Sometimes, in training, we refer to the concept of an emotional bank account to describe what happens in the relationship between people. If you ask a favour, or you make a decision that has a negative effect on someone else, then you make a withdrawal. If you do a favour for another person, or you give them a compliment, then you make a deposit. If your account as a leader is well balanced, then it is possible to make a big withdrawal, when it is necessary, to make a tough and unpopular decision. However, this is difficult if there is little or no money in the bank, so an important lesson for leadership is to make sure that there is. One way of doing this is applying the principles of the New Leadership ABCs, as explained later on.

In summary, to have a positive and effective relationship with the limbic brains of your employees, you have to:

- Respect people and their role (status).

- Make the world as predictable as you can.

- Give people a well-defined playing field with clear boundaries (certainty), where they have space to control and influence (autonomy).

- Make sure that everyone feels that they belong to the team. If you are not sure that someone fits your team, then take action and help this person to find another role.

- Keep an eye on the fairness of exchanges between you and your employees, and mutually between employees.

Exercise: Are You Respecting SCARF When Leading?

On **www.mindgrowing.net** you can donwload your personal development logbook. This is an interactive PDF in which you can insert your answers for every exercise in this book.

If you are leading according to SCARF then people should be moving towards you and voluntarily following you. If not, perhaps your employees are not as motivated and engaged as they could be. Perhaps you have identified one or more of the causes for this. You might ask for feedback from someone you trust, who dares to give you constructive criticism.

You should also take into account that these five elements can be respected without being absolutes. By this, I mean that people often expect and accept (depending on personality and national culture) a certain amount of difference in status, certainty, autonomy, relatedness, and fairness at work.

Use the following guiding questions to assess your leadership and your respect of the five SCARF elements in relation to your employees:

GUIDING QUESTIONS	GOING WELL	TO RECONSIDER OR TO IMPROVE
Status Do you treat them like adults? Do you avoid being too regulating or repressive? Are you too caring, solving all problems for them? Do you allow them to show their results and to be proud of them? Do you treat them as equally worthy to you? Do you follow exactly the same rules as them? Do you have exactly the same privileges as them? Do you earn more than seven times the lowest wage in your company?		
Certainty Are you informing them enough on what is going on? What is happening inside and outside the company, and how is it dealt with? What are the challenges and expectations that they have to deal with? Are the ambitions and the playing field clear and explicit?		

GUIDING QUESTIONS	GOING WELL	TO RECONSIDER OR TO IMPROVE
Autonomy Do you give them the space and freedom to decide what they can and need to do to realise the team's, the company's and their own ambitions? Are the ambitions and the playing field clear, so that they know their degrees of autonomy? Do you develop and inspire them to embrace their own autonomy and related accountability?		
Relatedness Does everyone in your team know that they are, without any doubt, part of the team? When someone is not fitting in with the team (for whatever reason), do you swiftly take action to give clarity? Do you invest in creating constructive working relationships between team members and in shaping a good atmosphere?		
Fairness Do you treat everyone in the same way (i.e. no favourites)? Is there a fair balance between giving and taking between you and employees, and amongst employees? Is everyone contributing according to their own capabilities? Are you rewarding, stimulating and developing everyone in a fair way? (E.g. a co-worker with high potential might receive different training, but that does not mean that no investment is needed for others.)		

Giving Meaning to Experience with Your Rational Brain

Figure 4.4 The Neo-cortex, highlighted in blue

Finally, let's go back to the timeframe of the development of our brain. Hours ago, we developed the crocodile and the limbic brain. A few seconds ago, a new part of the brain slowly developed called the neo-cortex. To simplify, the neo-cortex (our rational brain) is all about conscious and logic reasoning, planning, abstract thinking, and language. For me, one of the most important things the rational brain does is give meaning to everything we experience: seeing, feeling (tactile and emotional), hearing, and smelling.

However, one of the most important discoveries in emotional intelligence was that stimuli take a shortcut to the emotional brain. We previously thought that stimuli were first processed by the rational brain, and then sent to the emotional brain, to choose an appropriate emotion. More recent theories stress much more the continuous influence and interaction between the crocodile, emotional, and rational brain. Now there seems to be a consensus about the 'shortcut' to the emotional brain. One of the main functions of the crocodile brain is to scan all stimuli received, and to act when something is labelled as dangerous or interesting. The limbic brain does the same thing, but seems to be more focused on stimuli that give crucial positive or negative information concerning social survival. I would like to mention the SCARF elements again here, as I see them as the key components of social survival and well-being. I cannot stress enough that, when physical or social integrity (SCARF) is in danger, the crocodile and the limbic brain take charge and tend to put aside the rational brain. This happens when they feel that there is no time for rational analysis, and that immediate action is necessary to secure physical and/or social survival. I see that this often happens when SCARF elements are not respected by a leader. The leader's people often go into active (fight) or passive (flight) resistance. Or they just freeze and play dead. It is well known that when emotions take over your IQ drops 10 to 15 points. You can analyse many situations in a rational way and find all sorts of good reasons to do something but, if your limbic brain takes over, you may not be able to follow through.

For example, you want to give your leader some feedback because you think that he is too controlling and you feel smothered. Together with a colleague, coach, or your partner, you analyse this issue and you prepare a meeting. Rationally, you know what you want to say, and you know that you are right. You even practised with your partner the evening before. Then you are sitting in his office and your rational mind is already formulating the sentences inside your head. But when the limbic brain is triggered on the basis of its emotional memory (namely: a male authority figure + giving feedback = 'no good' and threatening for your social position) it takes action and it makes you freeze. What you rehearsed gets fuzzy in your head and you don't say what you wanted to. This fuzziness is what we call 'psychological mist', initiated by the limbic brain to protect you.

The rational brain is still occupied by survival but, again, it adds something new to the equation— it gives meaning to what is perceived in the external world, often together with what is felt inside. Giving meaning is a way to make the world predictable and controllable. The main function of the rational brain seems to be to make a consistent construction or representation of the inside and outside world. This construction helps to predict, anticipate, and manage the environment that we live in. Crucial to the rational mind is that everything is explainable, consistent, and that it all fits. If observations or new information of any kind don't fit with the construct made by the rational brain, then either the new information is ignored, or interpreted in such a way that it fits. In some instances, the brain also changes its construct of the world but, for this to happen, new and convincing information, which cannot be ignored, is needed. This means that once a construct is there it is not easily changed

Going back to the example of the mother that always gives negative feedback: your limbic brain already has an embedded message that a female authority figure equals a bad feeling. Your rational brain registers this bad feeling and it has to explain it or give it meaning. Keep in mind that in the first year of your life core emotional memories are constructed within the emotional brain. Then, when language and conscious thought kicks in, the rational brain has to find meaning for all those emotions felt. So, the rational brain only notices the feeling (certainly in early life, when there are no words), without being conscious about the reason for the feeling. It has to give its own meaning to the feeling.

From here, the rational brain can go different ways depending on the constructs already available and on information from other significant people. Parents and families transmit many of these labels and prefixed constructs to children. They are all part of the culture in which a child develops its rational brain. So, the rational brains of different children can label the felt emotion differently. One child may build a construct that ignores the relationship between the feeling and the behaviour of the mother, "It's just me feeling bad, it is my personality." This could be reinforced when you grow up within a culture where individual responsibility is promoted through different prefixed constructs. Another child will build a construct that ignores the feeling entirely, thinking, "It's all fantasy, it's not real, forget about it, push it away." This could happen when the dominant culture says that feelings are "bullshit" and "for wimps". Perhaps one child builds a construct that says, "Yes, my mother is a negative person, she makes me feel bad." This could perhaps be the case when you grow up in a culture that promotes a certain image of women. Still another will come to the conclusion that it is his own fault entirely, "I am stupid and always doing things wrong, so it is normal that my mother gives me negative feedback."

I believe it is here that the core of personality is created. The crocodile and the limbic brain are mainly occupied with physical and social survival. If you look at the psychology of early child development you will recognize the central emotional themes which are described as being relevant in this early development:

- Feeling safe.

- Being able to control own environment.

- Having a place within the group. Preferably the best, or at least a good position.

It is my hypothesis that the limbic brain mainly builds emotional constructs (emotion connected with a situation) based on these three core needs of the crocodile and limbic brain. These emotional constructs are the first drivers for behaviour in early life. Then, when thoughts and language develop, the rational brain starts labelling and giving meaning to these emotional constructs in relation to whatever it experiences in the external world. But the rational brain also has an influence on the limbic brain. The labelling of emotional constructs, when used consciously, can alter their effect. Although this does not seem to be easy, certainly not when emotional early life constructs are involved, there is increasing evidence that it is possible because the brain keeps developing throughout our entire life. For an extensive description of this see Daniel G. Amen's book Change Your Brain, Change Your Life. In his book, Amen explains that different parts of the brain can be overactive, underactive and/or dominant. For example, in some people, the limbic system is very sensitive and active. It keeps firing signals into the brain about feeling physically and socially unsafe. Amen calls this the creation of 'ANTs', or Automatic Negative Thoughts about oneself. He argues that these ANTs have to be killed by rational thinking and by writing down all the arguments against the negative thoughts.

For example, write down your ANTs:

- I am not intelligent enough to lead.

- People don't accept me.

- People are talking about me.

Then, every day, take some time to write counter arguments for these ANTs:

- I passed university with great results.

- Today, in a meeting, most people were enthusiastic about my proposal.

- I have no clue if people are talking about me. There is no factual evidence that they are.

Amen also writes about how a thought is something physical and real, electric stimuli fired in the brain. So, if you give negative thoughts the opportunity to keep on firing, then they will become stronger and more powerful. I strongly recommend having a look at his book. In it he describes, in more detail, the different parts of the brain, what happens when they are overactive or underactive, and how you can do something about it when needed.

Summary: Neuropsychology and the Development of Personality and Behaviour

The graph on the next page gives a visual representation of the dynamic forces induced by different parts of the brain which create your personality and identity. All this happens in order to make sense of the world internally and externally, so that it becomes predictable, and so that physical and social survival is realised. First, there are the crocodile and limbic brains (emotional mammal brain), constructing the first emotional impressions from which emotional drivers are constructed. They are mostly derived from the three basic human needs of being safe, being in control of your environment, and having a good position within the group. So, key drivers can be:

"I need to feel safer."

"I need to have more influence and control."

"I need to be popular, accepted, and have a good place in the group."

These emotional drivers produce constant impulses in the rational brain to develop a rational and predictable way to handle these drivers. And, don't forget, your environment and culture already offer many beliefs and constructs on how the world works and how things should be handled. This can make tackling your emotional drivers much more complicated. For example, if you have an emotional driver that says to you that you are not feeling safe, and you grow up in a culture where showing vulnerability is not accepted, you will suppress this feeling and build rational beliefs to convince yourself that you are safe. Your rational brain might develop an ego that says:

"I am strong."

"I don't care about what others think."

"I will not accept other people fooling me."

This tension between emotional drivers and rational constructs can cause even more feelings of discomfort during your life. But the opposite is also true. If you grow up in a culture or environment where you are encouraged to show vulnerability and emotions, you will be able to express your feelings of lack of safety, leading to a whole different set of rational beliefs and values. Your rational brain might construct an ego that says:

"I am a sensitive person, open to my own and others feelings."

"I encourage self-expression."

And, to be honest, both egos could either work well, or go to extremes and become destructive. The first ego could fight and be defensive, and the second ego might always push people to express emotions. All the rational constructs, built by your rational brain, will guide your behaviour. If you believe you have to defend yourself, then you will perhaps be argumentative, you will look for possible enemies, and you will prepare yourself for all kinds of threatening situations. If you believe that you are a sensitive person, then perhaps you will ask a lot of questions about how other people think and feel. In both cases the emotional trigger is the same, but, because of environment, the ego built is very different. This will lead to people showing completely different kinds of behaviour on the outside. And to make it even more complex, once the process of personality creation (at, or before birth) has started, all elements in play (emotional drivers, rationality creating beliefs and constructs, and behaviour) influence each other. So, emotional drivers can trigger the shaping of certain beliefs and rational constructs, but changing your rational way of thinking can also have an effect on your emotions. Emotions and beliefs will trigger behaviour, but changing your behaviour can also affect your emotions and beliefs. The fact that all of these elements influence each other gives us a lot of opportunities to trigger personal development. In my experience, personal development is key in developing all kinds of skills, and is most effective when you work on all levels. For instance, only working on behaviour without triggering the underlying beliefs can work, but is often a time-consuming and difficult process. Daring to touch all elements (emotions, beliefs, behaviour), delivers a more rapid and in-depth kind of development.

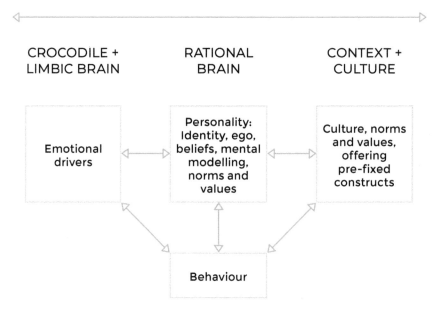

Figure 4.5 The dynamic internal and external forces that create our personality

You can only truly know an individual (if this is even possible), by investigating, in an open way, how these different elements came into play during their life, and how they formed their personality. This means that personality is a, more or less, arbitrarily made construction. And something that is constructed can also be deconstructed and reconstructed. Too often I hear, "Oh, but you can't expect me to change my personality!" When I started as a consultant, I always thought that, when people said this during training or coaching, I ought to respond with, "Of course not. You are who you are. You can change your behaviour, but not your personality." But I learned that changing your behaviour will eventually change your personality. People are very sensitive when you mention changes to their personality, and this is very understandable; the personality is the most fundamental compass we have to deal with the external world, and to build an identity. It is good to realise that, when one is holding on to personality, it could mean holding on to emotions, thoughts, beliefs, and behaviour that was once very useful but which is no longer. Sometimes it is even the opposite—it can become highly ineffective.

What I see happening often, is that we develop behaviour, convictions, and norms that were, at a certain point in our lives, very effective but, as we grow older and circumstances change, they often don't work anymore. For example, let's go back to the mother example (and I apologize to all mothers!) It is possible that, to avoid the negative feedback from your mother, you developed the conviction that everything must be well prepared and well thought out. In the relationship with your mother, this worked well, otherwise it would not have become a belief. So, you became a person who is always well organized, well prepared, and thoughtful. But now you are living in a world where you could benefit from spontaneity and improvisation; characteristics for which you constructed a dislike because they are inconsistent with other constructions of how you should be. Your strong focus on being well prepared and structured is now working against you, and your leader is not your mother! Your leader is expecting more improvisation and flexibility. You are often limiting yourself by holding onto your old, constructed personality, by saying that spontaneity and improvisation is not you. So why not change? You can, and it is your choice! Development never can, and should not be, imposed by other people.

What Does This All Mean for Leading People?

The world is changing rapidly and requires adaptability and flexibility, and therefore intrinsically motivated and engaged employees. Knowledge about the different parts of our brain, and how they function and interact in shaping the personality and motivation of people, gives us enormous insight on how to lead! This approach can be defined as neuroleadership.

Here is a summary of the key lessons in this chapter.

Respect SCARF (Status, Certainty, Autonomy, Relatedness and Fairness)
Make sure people want to follow you, and that they move towards you and not away. Use SCARF to stop people shifting into fight, flight, or freeze mode. When they do, they tend to lose 10 to 15 IQ points! It's your behaviour that can make a team smart or stupid.

Respect people, treat them as adults, listen, and use their perspective. Inform them about what is going on, and how you are dealing with issues. Give them the space to have initiative, ownership, and control over their own tasks. Say when something is not done as expected. Connect people to each other and build a team where everyone is involved and things are fair.

Look beneath the waterline
Build awareness and skill, to observe what is going on beneath the waterline, and inside people's hearts and minds. Our place in the pecking order is still important. While you may think you have a very rational ambition and approach, most people are going for safety, position, or control, and may not see it like that. Don't underestimate these drivers, as they can trigger ineffective behaviour, and ruin team dynamics and performance. Observe, detect them, and make them part of face-to-face or team talks. Intervene, and use your dominance to avoid too much struggle for position at the expense of others. Use the desire of the emotional brain to connect and to be part of an effective team to keep people on board. Give them time, and organise opportunities to connect and build trust.

Behaviour is emotion driven, so don't overestimate the importance of rationality
Remember that behaviour is initiated in the emotional brain, not in the rational brain. Free (rational) will only lasts for one tenth of a second.

So, people will not show the desired behaviour when they don't want to follow you as a leader. This happens when they don't trust you (they must feel, smell, and see that you are also defending their interests), and/or when they don't accept your dominance over them (so be decisive when key values are at stake, or relevant decisions need to be made). People will not work well together when there is no emotional and social connection. Again, time and occasion to bond, to connect, and to get to know each other, is essential.

Know the person behind the behaviour
People have an emotional memory, and often react to situations that happened far in the past. If a worker seems to be in an authority conflict with you, it could well be that it has absolutely nothing to do with you. They may be acting out an emotional pattern from their relationship with their father or mother. Being aware of this can help you to avoid reacting from the parent position (punish and blame them), which would feed the pattern. Instead, react as a rational adult, giving them clear expectations and feedback based on facts that are not emotionally driven. One can assume that a leader triggers a lot of emotional patterns created within the parent relationship.

Manage activity and passivity within your team dynamic
Facilitate the difference in levels of dominance and activity within the team. A team can only be effective and strong when there are leaders and followers. I always say that the amount of dominance should always be limited within a team. But the same goes for submission. The main risk is that a team easily gets stuck in fixed patterns, with the same people in the active and passive roles. This causes repetition, which fails to utilise everyone's competencies, and frustration all around. A good way to deal with this is to discuss this pattern, and to see if you can give different people more active leading roles, according to their competencies and fields of expertise.

To develop people, explore behaviour, beliefs, and feelings
Don't forget that, when you want to coach and/or develop people, personality behaviour is intertwined with beliefs and emotions. People will have the greatest opportunity to develop and grow when they have clear examples for new behaviour, when their beliefs and feelings are explored and taken seriously, and when the necessary support can be given to overcome hurdles at all levels.

CASE STUDY FOUR
The new CEO and his executive committee

I was once contacted by the CEO of a large chemical production factory. He wanted coaching for his executive committee, which he inherited from his predecessor. He found them to be passive, reactive, not truly engaged, and not speaking their minds. This is definitely not behaviour you would expect from executive leaders.

I asked the CEO if I could join a meeting with him and his team to observe their interactions. What I saw explained everything. It was a regular meeting, and it was set up in such a way that every member only needed to present on their own department. When they presented, almost all of them received negative remarks on what they were doing, and how they should do things differently, and this all came from the CEO. The whole team mostly kept quiet, only asking a few superficial questions they felt obliged to contribute, until it was their turn to talk. So, de facto, the CEO was running the show. The executive leaders were not feeling respected, had little or no autonomy, and did not feel any certainty, fairness, or connection to each other. In other words, the CEO was running his factory, but he was not building a team that could do the work for him. He put his team members in what we describe as a 'moving away from him' mode, instead of a 'let's approach' one.

Did the CEO have bad intentions? No. The main problem was that this man was so intellectually smart, quick and active! He really knew how to do things better and, based on his extensive experience, he had almost all the answers. But what he was lacking was emotional intelligence, and more specific knowledge about the way our human brain functions. He did not realise that, when you don't respect one of the oldest parts of the brain, namely the emotional or mammal brain, then it will take control and put people in 'moving away' mode (flight or freeze). When this happens, the IQ of people tends to drop 15 to 20 points, so he was literally making his team stupid. But, luckily, rational intelligence can also help to tap into emotional intelligence. After a few coaching sessions with him, and a facilitated dialogue between him and his team, things took a turn in the right direction and improved drastically.

The brain is the only organ that studies itself.

Prof. Dr. Jean-Pierre De Waele

PART III:

The New Leadership ABCs

In the previous chapters I described what I see as the context and basis for future leadership. On one hand, there is the rapidly changing world, which will ask more of leadership than management. We need leadership that creates a high level of adaptability; leadership that develops people who are competent to act in a professional way when faced with rapidly changing circumstances. Leaders also need to engage employees in the most effective way possible, namely by emotional attachment. Emotional attachment happens when people feel connected to their company and are willing and engaged to do their best, not only because they are paid for it, but because they feel truly respected. This will only be possible when a culture is created that fully understands and fosters the intrinsic motivation of people.

American author Daniel Pink collected a massive pool of scientific evidence that shows that the 'carrot and stick' approach to motivating people only works when people are performing simple, mechanical tasks. The moment that a minimal amount of critical, creative thinking is required, it no longer works. Pink tells us, as we have known for a long time, that earning more money is not a motivator. However, when people are not paid according to market standards it will act as a disincentive; a demotivator. This means that the lack of good pay will constantly be on people's minds. So, the best way to deal with this is to take money off the table by paying a fair salary. There is no need to reach beyond what is 'fair,' as Pink tells us there is a lot of evidence to demonstrate that more money and big bonuses seldom improve performance.

Recent brain research shows us that to reach a high level of engagement, and to tap into the intrinsic motivation of people, it is crucial to have a high level of respect. This is encapsulated in the SCARF principles. As a leader, you have to make sure that the need for status, certainty, autonomy, relatedness, and fairness is respected. The ABCs of future leadership offer a clear and structured framework that help you to put all the above principles into practice. It describes the three main things that you, as a leader, have ultimate responsibility to make sure are clearly formulated: ambition, boundaries, and coaching. These three things create a thriving partnership with your employees, and create clear expectations and high demands at both ends of the partnership (leaders and employees). It does not mean that you have to define or execute the three elements all by yourself. Depending on the level of maturity of your team, you can and must consult and involve team members in reflection and discussion about the ambition, the boundaries, and the way in which coaching and development is organised. But it should always be you who takes the lead, the responsibility for the global process, and the end result.

CHAPTER FIVE

Understanding Your Drivers, Beliefs and Ego

In this chapter, I focus mainly on getting to know yourself better, and discovering the main drivers of your emotional needs, values, beliefs, and ego. This is because I believe it is the best way to formulate an ambition that is authentic and gets to the core of who you are. I will offer several reflection tools to help you explore your inner self and how it determines your current ambition and behaviour.

In the last part of the chapter I will make a sharp turn towards how to formulate, based on an authentic ambition, effective business goals for a team, department, or company.

Knowing Yourself: Your Emotional Drivers, Rational Beliefs, Values and Ego

First, there has to be an ambition. Something you are willing to work for; something you want to realise, create, or shape. And it cannot be making money. As British-American author and motivational speaker, Simon Sinek, stated in one of his talks, "Money is a result, not a purpose, or ambition." The challenge is to formulate an ambition that answers the question, "Why do you get out of bed in the morning and spend your days toiling away in this organisation?" For me, there is no leadership if there is no ambition to lead people to a better place, be it physically, emotionally, psychologically, or otherwise.

Ambition must come from the heart. And, by heart, I mean emotions. It is rooted in what you deeply feel to be worthwhile goals to achieve.

You only can truly engage people if they feel that your ambition is based on authentic feelings. When this is the case, you will communicate on the level of the limbic brain, which is the most able to engage other people on an emotional level, therefore creating real passion between you.

The limbic brain does not know words and numbers. It will, however, observe your behaviour and listen to your tone of voice when you are talking about your ambition. It immediately notices if what you are saying is honest and real. If it senses honesty and realness it will build trust and people will follow. I am strongly convinced that it is impossible to do the inverse, namely convince people with rational arguments to get on board with an ambition or goal that you don't feel is valuable. You might be able to force them for a while, but the real intrinsic motivation will not be there, and the results will be poor.

So, in order to formulate an inspiring ambition, you have to know yourself and you need to feel the emotions in your heart. That's why, in this chapter, I will spend a lot of time on how to gain insight into the different layers of your personality.

This is also true for the people you lead. It is equally important that they can relate the ambition to their own values and feelings. That is why it is so crucial to involve people, as much as possible, in defining the ambition. Take time for it; say what you want to attain; ask people what they want and feel; and try to combine these in order to find the exciting ambition for the team, department, or company. If you estimate that people are not yet mature or competent enough for this type of discussion, then involve them slowly, step-by-step, and develop them in this direction. Chapter Eleven explores basic structures to shape this interaction with employees.

Your leading ambition has to be connected to your heart. It has to be anchored to your core values and drivers in order to be real. That is why I want to elaborate on how to get a hold of your own drivers: the values, emotions, and beliefs that steer your behaviour.

How to Get a Hold on Your Core Emotional Drivers

The best way to get insight into your emotional drivers is to peel back the different layers of your personality. The core of who you are (your key values) is often wrapped in other layers, which all together form your ego. The ego is a coat you put on, during your development as a person, to defend and/or position yourself to the outside world. It also often acts as a kind of protection for strong internal emotions or perceived vulnerabilities. The coat is often so thick that you lose touch with your essence. That's why peeling the layers back, or stripping off the ego, can be so important and valuable.

During my experience as a coach I developed an approach that explains the different layers, the interaction between them, and how to work with this concept to learn more about yourself and your core drivers. Later on, I will provide an exercise to guide you through these levels, in order to provide more clarity on how they might work for you.

The illustration below represents the different layers of personality and the interaction between them. This concept is an integration of neuroleadership and concepts like the psychological levels initiated by Gregory Bateson and defined by Robert Dilts, as well as work by Bas Blekkingh on authentic leadership.

Let me first explain the different layers in more detail, together with an example, going from the outside environment to your internal world. I will describe the different layers from the perspective that you want to develop yourself. In that light, each level has its own striking questions. Development and change are possible on each level. First, I will describe the nature of the different levels and, afterward, I will explain the arrows and the lines in the graph representing the inter- and extra-personal dynamics.

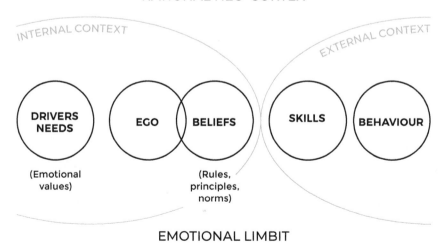

Figure 5.1 The different layers of personality and the interaction between them

Context and How you Perceive It

Your context is the environment in which you work or live, and also specific situations you encounter. For example, suppose you get a lot of questions from colleagues for help on a variety of things. You would like to say no, but you don't. Important questions to ask are, "What is your perception of this situation?" and "How do you think and feel about the situation, your colleagues, and their questions?" I intentionally use the word 'perception' here. In Chapter Four I wrote about neuroleadership and how the rational brain makes a representation of the world, but also how this representation is never objective. Your rational brain gives meaning to everything it perceives, and it perceives things in a selective way. It is important, on this level, to disconnect the meaning you assign to things from the facts as they really happen. Sometimes this can solve or at least redefine a problem. For example, if you think that colleagues deliberately take advantage of you, then they are the problem. On the other hand, if you think they are simply nice people and you don't have an issue with them taking advantage of you, then you are the problem for not creating boundaries. So, depending on your perception, and the meaning you give to a situation, the problem will change.

Behaviour

This is what you literally do, say, feel, or think in a certain situation or context. Following the example above, when approached by colleagues for help, you might say to yourself, "When I panic, I feel disturbed, and I think 'I have so much to do, and I don't have the time to help them, but I feel awkward saying no.'" As a result, you say, "OK, no problem. I can do that for you." The most important question you can ask yourself is whether you want or need to do something different.

Knowledge and Skills

What is the knowledge and what are the skills you have that allow you to express this behaviour? In this case, what is the knowledge and what are the skills that allow you to think and feel what you do, and to say, "Yes, I can do that for you"? This can consist of different things. In this case, here are some possibilities:

- You can control your emotion (you don't show panic).

- You have knowledge about social rules (you can't always say no).

- You have the skills to put someone else's needs above yours.

The most important message here is that, whatever you do, there are always skills involved. No matter how negative you perceive a certain behaviour, it always implies useful skills. The important question to ask yourself is whether there are any skills demonstrated you can develop or use in another way.

Beliefs

We often carry rules, assumptions, and cognitive constructs that say how the world works and how things must go. Here are some examples of contrasting rules:

- You must always be on time or being on time is not important.

- You must have an eye for detail or details are not important.

- People need safety or people need to be confronted.

In our example, the ruling belief could be that you have to help your colleagues because you must always be loyal to people close to you, and it is not polite to say no. Norms are often black and white. They are a condensed summary of how you think the world works, or has to work. Beliefs can also be unconscious and are often based on emotional constructs. As described in Chapter Four, an emotional construct is an emotional memory constructed in the limbic brain. For example, when you encountered situations where you said no, often as a child, and you perceived strong negative consequences. The limbic brain then remembers saying no brings about a bad feeling. So, in situations where something is asked and rationally you would like to say no, the limbic brain acts on past bad feelings and pushes you to say yes. The unconscious feeling makes you say yes, not some conscious rule telling you to do so. It is not unusual that the conscious and emotional (unconscious) norms conflict. For example, rationally you construct the norm that a strong person has to be able to say no, while the emotional norm keeps giving you the bad feeling when you do. The good news is that they influence each other. Becoming rationally aware of this can help to change the emotional belief.

An important question to ask here is whether there are any rational or emotional beliefs that are blocking you. Are they effective or are they holding you back? At the moment beliefs are established, they are always effective in some way. However, later on in your life, as circumstances change, they can become very ineffective. You might feel that your beliefs are important, and that they are supporting you in giving clarity and structure about how the world works or has to work, which is true. But you also need to have a critical look at them. They may also be holding you back because they are stored as black and white constructs, without flexibility. Furthermore, they could also be responsible for conflicts and the tendency to over-control and micromanage.

Whenever people fight and make war it is because of conflicting beliefs, and not necessarily because of conflicting values. Beliefs are values translated into rules. Most people around the world have the same values, but have different rules to convey them into behaviour. For example, having respect for others is a commonly shared value in most societies and cultures. However, in one culture you might show respect by looking someone in the eyes, and in another culture is very disrespectful to do so. So, beliefs are man-made constructs and in that sense they are arbitrary.

The Ego
The ego is the image of yourself that you (often unconsciously) present to the external environment, and often also to yourself. You have learned, felt, or experienced that a certain coherent repertoire of beliefs, values and behaviours are effective to realising your emotional drivers. This repertoire of behaviours can often be characterised by being a certain type of person:

- The intellectual observer, keeping his distance.

- The loyal friend you can always count on.

- The performer, always ambitious and focused on results.

- The funny one, always looking for a laugh.

In our example, when you say yes to everyone's requests, you may be presenting yourself as the loyal and trustworthy colleague. Beliefs, values, and ego are strongly related. A certain ego leads to a certain set of beliefs. If you see yourself as the loyal and trustworthy person people can count on, then it is likely that you translate this into all kinds of beliefs and values. You will create a set of rules that define what you need to do to be loyal and trustworthy. One rule could be that, if you are loyal, you never say no. Saying no means you are no longer loyal to someone. As you can see, all of this is very subjective. Is it really true that by saying no in this situation you're showing a lack of loyalty? And if it is, is it always true? When is it and when is it not?

The ego is a coat you have woven, both consciously and unconsciously, often to reconcile what you feel about what you do. Looking at our example, on the inside you want to say no but at the same time it gives you a bad feeling, so you say yes. There is a discrepancy with at least one drive, the desire to stand up for yourself. Your rational mind needs to explain this to make the world predictable. So, the ego (the coat) is created, as if to say, "You know me, I am a loyal and trustworthy person, so I say yes out of principle, because loyalty is a core value of mine." This avoids you having to say, "I say yes for the simple reason that I am just too afraid to say no." This would be too vulnerable and is unsafe for the brain. Vulnerability is a difficult concept for us human beings. For our crocodile and limbic brain, showing vulnerability is a no go. The danger for physical or social survival is enormous. When the possible opportunity to eat and mate is linked to the position you take in the group it feels like suicide to present yourself as weak.

As consultants, executive coaches, and trainers, we work a lot on this topic and try to convince leaders to show some vulnerability. They often ask why this is so important. It is important because it can create amazing results. This is exactly where our human potential is. It creates authenticity because there is no longer a need to keep up appearances, which cost a huge amount of energy. This, in turn, builds trust because people know that what they see is real and not an act. It's as if you take off your coat and attach less importance to your ego.

Don't misunderstand me, we need our egos. They are not necessarily negative. Like all these mechanisms, they help us to function and to make the best of our lives. My main point is that often they become too strong, making all kinds of beautiful things impossible. But we can become aware of these problems and we can change. Animals can't. You remember Mike, the chimp bashing his cans, pretending that he is the alpha male. He has to continue bashing those cans long after the novelty has worn off and he is fed up with it. Eventually, the other chimps will discover that it's just an act. Sadly, Mike might have little choice in adjusting his behaviour, but we do. We can create interactions and relationships where it is possible to take off our old worn-out coats and show some vulnerability. Most of the time it leads to more authenticity, trust, and unleashes enormous creative potential.

Emotional Drivers and Values

Emotional drivers and values are the energy coming from different parts of the brain that drive you to act and think. This energy originates in the needs of our brain. It's these needs of the limbic brain, in early life, that determine the core of our drivers. They form the grains of your personality. The brain mainly has two kinds of needs:

1. Those coming from fear: Protecting physical and social survival i.e. the need to be safe; the need to be in the group, not outside; the need for fairness; the need for predictability and structure (including the need for leadership); the need to have control.

2. Those coming from a desire to progress: Improving physical and social positions i.e. the need to have better or safer living conditions; the need to save energy; the need for a higher status or position.

The rational brain finds a way to construct an ego in order to deal with these emotional drivers. So, these basic needs I see as the origin of our ambitions. These needs are very fundamental and often not easy changeable. Depending on your upbringing, life history, and your circumstances, primarily during your early life, this can be very different. For example, if you always felt very safe, then safety is probably is not a driver for you, and vice versa. Objective circumstances can play a role, but even more important is what the brain feels and perceives. For example, a child might grow up in objectively unsafe circumstances, but may not perceive it that way. This person will feel safe. The inverse is also possible: a child might grow up in a very safe environment but still feel unsafe. Similarly, if a need for fairness is not fulfilled, or becomes, in some other way, an emotional issue, then fairness will probably become one of your core values. Core emotions, core needs, and core values are three variations of the same thing.

Appendix: Phases of Child Development and Possible Developmental Drivers of the Ego describes the different phases of child development, showing how different needs can become drivers within different phases, leading to different kinds of egos. This could be a source of inspiration if you want to reflect upon your own personality, and on those of the people you lead.

Now I will describe the lines and the arrows from Figure 5.1, representing the way in which all layers interact in a dynamic way.

Interaction Between the Layers of Personality

Emotional drivers are the basic needs of the brain but, depending on the context and the way you perceive the context, one driver can become more important than another. Some examples include:

- If you grew up in an unsafe environment, the need for safety might become a strong driver.

- If you grew up in a family with seven or eight children, the need for position and status might be a strong driver.

- If your parents were very controlling, the need for control might be a strong driver.

But the way you perceive your environment is crucial. Maybe you perceive your parents as being over-controlling, while others experience the same behaviour very differently.

The limbic brain can initiate behaviour directly, based on a need or drive. This is the case in our example, where a colleague said yes while he wanted to say no. The behaviour in this case is not triggered by ego, norms, or skills, but directly by an emotion. Changing your behaviour can also change your feelings. If you can steer your behaviour and say no a few times, and see that it works, then after a while your feelings will also change because of the positive experiences. You will have to review the message from your ego that says, "That's the person I am, loyal and trustworthy, but able to say no when it is really not possible."

To a large extent, emotional drivers create the ego and the norms. The ego and beliefs are a coat you weave, trying to fulfil your needs. But your ego and norms are also created through a strong interaction with the environment and culture you live in. If you live in an Asian country where saying no is not acceptable, then this will influence the development of your ego and norms. There is the strong desire to say no, but perhaps your ego has evolved to say, "Yes, that's me. I love my culture and I am well adapted, that's why I say yes." Again, it is all a matter of constructed and more or less arbitrary interplay between different elements of the personality.

Once the ego and the beliefs become established, they can initiate behaviour and develop skills. The effect of this behaviour will influence the ego and the norms. Suppose that, within the frame of my family, I develop the ego of being a loyal and trustworthy man, giving and creating trust. I have developed beliefs that tell me that saying no is not loyal; being loyal is offering help and agreeing with what other people say. These are the norms of my family, which I have integrated into my behaviour. So, I develop skills in the sense that I follow and agree with others easily. I develop this structure because, within my family, it helped me to fulfil my need for belonging in the group. Imagine that I now get my first job, and I arrive in a different context. I decide to use and elaborate the same skills. During my first review with my boss he says that I am too much of a follower and, if this doesn't change, I will not make it in this job. If this happens repeatedly, and I become aware that what I think doesn't work anymore, I have to change my belief and develop other skills. This will also lead to rational reframing of my ego. However, some people don't change their skills or their beliefs in these situations. They change their perception of the context i.e., "My boss is stupid," or their ego, "I am a loyal and trustworthy man, but misunderstood by so many."

This is an ongoing process during our lives (but with a crucial importance for early life), whereby all these elements are striving to align and shape a consistent whole of feelings, norms, convictions, and behaviour that fit within the environment and get us what we want.

All layers can be unconscious and below the surface. But you can be conscious of your needs, ego, beliefs, skills and behaviours. Self-reflection, coaching, training and feedback can make the unconscious parts conscious. It is the first step in changing whatever you want to change. You give more power to the rational brain, allowing it to oversee what is happening, and enabling it to have more conscious control over all elements.

Walking Through Yourself: A Way to Explore Your Personality and Drivers

There are two different approaches you can use to explore the different layers of your personality, including drivers. The first is a self-reflection exercise in which I will guide you, with questions and examples, through the different layers. The second is what I call mirroring: you interview someone else about yourself, using them as a mirror. The first is recommended when you first want to experiment on your own with these concepts, or when you don't have anyone to interview about yourself. Working alone requires strong and critical self-reflection, and honesty towards oneself. The second approach is interesting because you will get someone else's opinion. After all, the ego is a kind of defence mechanism, so it is not always capable of analysing itself. When you use the mirroring approach you should find someone who knows you well, who can be critical, and who you trust.

Exercise: Approach One, Auto-Reflection

When you do this, I recommend you write the different layers on pieces of paper and put them on the floor. This will give you the opportunity to really physically walk through them. What you see below are the layers. Next to them are some instructions and questions to ask yourself, then an example answer, and finally some space to write your own insights and conclusions. It is always advisable to do the exercise focusing on one typical behaviour within one specific situation. While you might think that this will give you limited insight into the layers of your personality, doing the exercise will trigger broader insights beyond the one example used. And, of course, it is also good to do the same analysis for a few key behaviours in key situations. If you really want to dive in deeper, it is good to get the advice of a trainer or coach.

Answer the following questions, one by one. Don't read all of the questions first, as this will influence the answers you give:

Think of a situation, combined with a behaviour, that demonstrates your character. First, describe what you see as crucial characteristics of the situation: where are you, with whom, what are the circumstances, and what are the characteristics of the people and the situation? This might be a situation where you show a behaviour with which you are not very pleased.

INSTRUCTION	EXAMPLE	YOUR SITUATION: Note the answers to the different questions.
CONTEXT		
Describe the situation and the people present.	Me, years ago: the evening before my first session of executive coaching.	
BEHAVIOUR		
What did you feel, think, and do in this situation?	I was nervous, insecure, and worried about how I would be perceived i.e. if it would 'click' and the people being coached would accept me. I went through several scenarios of what could happen and how I should react. I talked about these worries with my partner.	
SKILLS		
To show this behaviour, what are the skills and knowledge you demonstrate?	Imagination: making up all kind of scenarios. Able to communicate my worries to my partner. I take things seriously and I want to do things well. I prepare well. Self-reflection and self-criticism.	

INSTRUCTION	EXAMPLE	YOUR SITUATION: Note the answers to the different questions.
BELIEFS		
What makes you show this behaviour? In the case of the example, what makes you nervous and worried, and go through all kinds of scenarios? In other words, why not just be relaxed? Also, consider that some norms are emotional. Try to describe what you feel when thinking of the situation.	I believe coaching a CEO is quite a challenge because I believe that they are dominant people and I also believe that I am not. I believe that dominant people often show no respect for less dominant ones. I believe that dominant people don't accept mistakes and that they will blame and disregard you for them. I believe that the best way to avoid mistakes is to mentally prepare for all possible scenarios. I believe I have little experience. I believe it would be a huge failure if he didn't want to start the coaching after this first meeting. I believe I have an issue with dominance and this will block me during the interview. Note: The strength of this exercise is that, by writing "I believe" so often, in my mind I start labelling a lot of those beliefs as disputable, with the potential to change.	Use "I believe..." as often as you can.

INSTRUCTION	EXAMPLE	YOUR SITUATION: Note the answers to the different questions.
EGO		
This will probably be the hardest question to answer. You might want to ask someone else to read the answers you have just given to the previous question and then ask them to answer the following: which role are you playing here?	I feel I am playing the role of a submissive, well-behaved boy, creating a self-image of not being dominant and not being accepted by dominant people. This is a kind of protection I use in case I fail. I am already rationalising why the talk will go wrong, and I am spending a lot of energy thinking about and fixing things that may never happen.	
DRIVERS		
Again, perhaps ask for the help of someone that knows you well and whom you trust. Your drivers fuel your ego (your coat): what purpose is your ego serving, or, in other words, what vulnerability is it protecting?	The need to be accepted by alpha males and to be valued by them. I know that this is an emotional need coming from my childhood, when I perceived my father as being very dominant and not valuing me. So, the purpose of my ego here is to prepare me for another disappointment of not being valued.	

From this exercise, I now know that one of my core drivers is that I feel a lack of acceptance and of being highly valued by alphas. It will trigger me to keep doing things in order to gain the acceptance of those people and/or to build an ego explaining that I don't need it. So, does this help me to make progress? I think knowing your drivers is important, but understanding your ego and beliefs is also very valuable. They are the channel through which you can learn to cope with your drivers, in order to avoid emotional pain and disappointment. They deliver you a lot of positive things (for example, I developed a hard-working attitude to please dominant people), but they can also steer your behaviour in such a way that no longer makes sense.

How Understanding Your Drivers Will Help You Formulate an Authentic Ambition

When my ego gets the upper hand in defining my ambition, then there is a high chance that I will formulate an ambition that is pleasing an alpha. For example, an ambition which would enable the realisation of someone's vision. This doesn't have to be a problem, but I've noticed that it does not give me a lot of energy. When I take the other path and I start from my core driver, namely getting acceptance and being valued by alphas like my father, then I can tap in to this feeling and energy and discover what this really means to me. I noticed that, because of this driver, I always feel a strong emotional and compassionate connection with the underdog, with the people that don't get valued and respected by other more dominant people. I am so strongly convinced that a lot of these people, apparently not very motivated, could blossom when led differently. So, this has become my core ambition: to help create leadership that unleashes the energy and passion of many people. I shifted from striving for all kinds of ambitions aimed at pleasing alphas, to using this same energy to formulate an ambition for myself that feels good. Writing this book about the New Leadership ABCs is just one way to do this.

Exercise: Approach Two, Mirroring

Mirroring is seeing yourself reflected in the minds of others. The information you will get is highly valuable in shaping your personal development as a leader. Mirroring means that, by use of a structured interview, you gather information about the different layers in your personality by interviewing other people about how they perceive you.

Choose one or two people who are close to you and with whom you have a strong relationship. Choose two very different types of people (different personalities; different relationships with you; some being very critical, some very loving; some professional, some private). Choose people you find most relevant at this point in your life or career.

- Tell them that you want to work on your personal development as a leader and that you would appreciate it if they could take some time to help you, for approximately one to one and a half hours.

- Tell them that this help will be in the form of a one-on-one interview, with you interviewing them about yourself.

- Stress the fact that this is an interview and not a discussion or exchange. The only thing you will do is ask questions, listen, and ask some more questions to make sure that you understand what is being said. Stick to this approach! Don't start a discussion. You are asking for their perception, so accept it as it is.

- Record the interview and listen to it a few days later. Write down responses and mark what is most touching or striking to you.

Interview questions

Ask all of the questions in the order presented. Listen, and ask for examples to make things specific. Once again: Don't argue. Perception is perception. If a question is difficult to answer, ask them to compare you with other people and to tell you how you seem to act, think, or operate compared to others. They don't have to mention who the other people are. This is only a technique to help, and to provide a contrast, to allow them to describe your behaviours.

QUESTIONS	WRITE DOWN THE ANSWERS THAT STAND OUT TO YOU
Can you describe things I do and say which you find typically me? Please be as specific as possible, and give some examples of typical situations where I show this behaviour.	
Related to the behaviour you described, what do you see as my typical strengths? What kind of knowledge and skills do I have, to be able to show this behaviour?	
What rules and principles do you consider to be very important to me? Those that, when violated, would make me angry, sad, frustrated, etc.	

QUESTIONS	WRITE DOWN THE ANSWERS THAT STAND OUT TO YOU
What are my pet subjects, beliefs, and rules that always seem to be stressing me out and that I often talk about?	
Think of my behaviour and the beliefs, rules, and values which you consider to be important to me: Could you please try to capture all of this by describing it as a role that I am playing? **Note:** give time to reflect. If it is too difficult to answer, you can give some examples of what *could* be roles that demonstrate these i.e. The nice person, helping everyone; The tough person, beating everyone in a competition; The special person, different from all others.	

QUESTIONS	WRITE DOWN THE ANSWERS THAT STAND OUT TO YOU
What do you think are my vulnerabilities or insecurities that I have deep down? I do have them, I am just wondering if you can see or feel them? **Note:** Give time to think and reflect. If it is too hard, ask these questions in stead: 1. Do you see or feel any of my uncertainties? Which ones? 2. Do you feel that there are important things of which I am afraid? 3. In your eyes, do you feel I need to be in control of certain things? 4. Do you see me acting? What kind of need do you think I am fulfilling for myself in this (e.g. winning, being special, helping people, being on top of things?)	

Reflections and Conclusions

The following questions are very important. They will help you to consolidate and apply your learning in this chapter.

What are the core emotional drivers, beliefs, and egos you can identify in yourself?

EMOTIONAL NEEDS/DRIVERS	BELIEFS, RULES, VALUES	EGOS i.e. roles you are playing

Are your beliefs and egos the most optimal way to deal with your emotional drivers? And, more importantly, are they fulfilling your needs and drives? Read the example I gave about myself in the auto-reflection approach, and see if you think the ego and beliefs I developed are effective in becoming highly valued by alpha people? To be honest, no, rather the opposite. Once in my life this worked, not anymore.

I call this the vicious belief trap. As an example, I want to be heard and I believe that this will happen if I use good arguments. So, every time I talk to someone, I am well prepared and I use a lot of arguments. However, they don't seem to listen! Acting on my belief, I look for more and stronger arguments to make my point. Perhaps, at a certain moment, you become aware (or not) that people are avoiding you. Without realising it, you get the opposite of what you need; people are avoiding you and you are not being heard. Look at yourself: do you recognize these kinds of vicious circles? Do you see other ways to act upon your core emotional drivers? It might also be wise to share this with someone and ask for advice.

To what extent are your ego and beliefs blocking others? Suppose I am a leader. I am most likely converting all my own beliefs into rules, which have to be followed by people with completely different beliefs. This could weigh heavily on the engagement and motivation they have. Where do you see your own emotional needs, beliefs, and ego having an effect on others?

Reflecting on emotional drivers, beliefs, and ego, and having thought about them in the sense of whether or not they are helping, try to keep the energy of each driver, but reformulate it into a new ambition that relates to the core of your being.

In Chapter Six I will give you some thoughts on how to formulate business goals with this core ambition as a foundation.

How core values don't have to change but can be reframed towards different behaviours

Catherine was struggling with her leadership. Her own manager said that she was not strict and dominant enough to push her employees towards results. He found she didn't provide clear instructions and no-nonsense follow through. The department was doing poorly and got a lot of internal complaints for not delivering the agreed results. Also, her team members felt lost and thought they were sailing on a sinking ship. Catherine attempted to imitate the style of her boss and tried to be strict, instructive and controlling. She felt very bad about it as this was going against her own personal drivers and values. She believed that the role of a leader is mainly to support and coach employees in doing a good job. During the coaching it became clear that her basic emotional drive to be accepted by others was translated into an ego that centred around being a helpful and supportive person. We investigated her beliefs about what it means to be a supportive and helpful person in more depth and, even more crucially, what it means to be a helpful and supportive leader! It was then that she discovered that being helpful and supportive as a leader means that you do have to give structure, instructions, follow-through, and coaching. In this way, she could link this behaviour to her core values and drivers. From that moment, she started learning the right skills, and she put them into practice. Behaviour that had felt unnatural and unpleasant to her, became realistic and useful by reframing it in the light of her core values, namely being a supportive and helpful leader.

Life is like riding a bicycle. To keep your balance you must keep moving.

Albert Einstein

CHAPTER SIX

Formulating a Business Ambition

Next to your ambition, which is based on passion coming from emotional drivers, there are two other things to consider. These are the competencies you have (what things are you really good at?), and the current and future economic situation (what are people willing to pay money for, now and/or in the future?). These three elements are nicely reflected in the 'Hedgehog Concept', from Jim Collins' book Good to Great. When you are able to find the interface between these three aspects you will be, as an individual as well as an organisation, happy and successful at the same time. This is called the 'Hedgehog Concept' because this animal has one core thing which is truly in its nature (its passion), one thing it does very well (its talent), and one thing that works perfectly in its environment; rolling up into a ball.

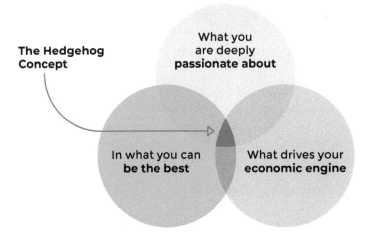

Figure 6.1 The Hedgehog Concept

In the previous sections, I have written about finding your true passion by getting to know yourself. This is featured in the circle, "What are you deeply passionate about?" Now, let's have a short look at the other two circles.

At What Can You Be the Best in The World?

This is about the strengths you have. And, to be honest, they are often related to your basic drives. You can imagine that, if your drive is to create identity through helping others, in developing your ego or 'coat', you also develop a lot of skills in relation to this. Thus, you have probably learned to be sensitive to the needs of others, to ask questions, to communicate well with people, and so on.

The same goes for developing this at team and organisational level. For example, the drive to help others may translate into developing a strategy of customer intimacy (i.e. being close to the customers and their needs is the crucial focus point to develop the business). If this choice to pursue customer intimacy is really genuine, and based on an authentic driver, then it is very likely that you have developed all kinds of skills, structures, and procedures that make you an expert in being close to the customer. It is important to keep in mind that these skills can be learned on an individual level, as well as on an organisational level, although it will demand quite an investment in time and money if it is too far away from your current skills. A core ambition, however, is almost impossible to learn or to fake; this must come from your drives. Also, it can be frustrating and a waste of time to always focus on improving weaknesses, where often there are a lot of strengths not used to their full potential. An instrument I really like using to define my own strengths is CliftonStrengths from Gallup.

What is My Economic Engine?

This is what people or companies want to pay money for. To investigate this, you have to do the necessary market research on how your potential market will perceive certain services and products, and if they are appealing enough to pay the right amount of money for.

Formulating Engaging Goals

When you have clarity about your deep ambitions, your present strengths and the ones that could be developed, and their feasibility in terms of economic profitability, then it is time to translate all of this into business goals. Below I offer you some tips and rules to formulate goals in such a way that they will keep the authenticity of your ambition and have the power to engage others.

It Has to be Output, Not Input

According to Filip Vandendriessche, author of Leading Without Commanding, the core aspect of an engaging goal is that it has to be output and not input. What is the difference?

Output is the desired relevant, tangible results that you want to accomplish in the short, mid or longterm. Key words are:

Relevant: The goal has to cover a certain basic need, which is hard to question. For example, better quality, state-of-the-art products, effective working, higher customer satisfaction, a better living for people, a better and more beautiful world.

Tangible result: The goal must say what you have created when it is realised, for example: The quality will be higher, employee satisfaction will increase, we will have a new state-of-the-art product, we will increase efficiency and effectiveness, we will have higher customer satisfaction, we will decrease stress for people.

However, many goals within companies are defined as input goals, in the sense that the goal describes the means and way (solution) to achieve the goal.

Let me give a simple example. A minister of traffic formulates the goal to limit speed on motorways to 100 km/hour. The goal incorporates a solution: to lower maximum speed. The latter, however, is not relevant and tangible to the end result. What is really important is a serious decrease in mortal accidents. Therefore, we typify this goal as an input (solution) goal. To achieve the output goal, which is fewer fatal accidents, you can lower the maximum speed, construct a roundabout, educate younger drivers about the risks of drinking and driving, take away distracting billboards, etc. Formulation of a goal in output terms leaves room for autonomy and mastery in finding the appropriate solution and addressing the real issue at stake.

A rule of thumb is to ask "so that?" or "in order to?" As long as you can do this, in an intellectually honest way, then you are still on the input level and are talking about solutions. So, if someone says, "My goal is to lower the speed on the motorway," you can ask, "In order to do what?", or, "So that what happens?" The person will probably say, "In order to decrease fatal accidents." Now you have the output goal. I borrowed the term "intellectually honest" from Fillip Vandendriessche. I use it because you can always keep asking why. Even when I say I want to decrease mortal accidents, someone could ask, "So that what happens?" But I hope you feel that this would not be an intellectually honest question. This is why an output goal is often so engaging, also on a limbic level. It relates very strongly to the basic drivers we described earlier like safety, control and position. Input goals, which are often more solutions than goals, relate to the ego or 'coat' you built i.e. you learned or constructed the conviction that this is a 'good solution', but the solution could be very different for other people. It reflects rules and norms, "The way to lower fatal accidents is to drive slower", rather than a goal.

The importance of formulating output goals is also that you, as a leader, explicitly indicate to your employees what is expected of them in terms of what to realise or create, while at the same time giving them responsibility and freedom for realising this output goal in their own manner i.e. the input or solution.

Here are some more examples:

INPUT GOAL (= SOLUTION)		OUTPUT GOAL (= END RESULT)	SMART OUTPUT GOAL
Install a new procedure for quality control by the end of next year.	So that	...we have good quality and less returns of our product.	...by the end of the year the return of products has dropped from 20 per cent to 2 per cent.
Within two months all documents must be alphabetically filed.	So that	...we can find a document quickly.	...we can find a document within three minutes.
By the end of May, I must complete a course in negotiating skills.	So that	...I can realise more of my interests.	...at the end of this year management has assured me that we are going to invest €200,000 in the development of our sales staff.

Figure 6.2 Examples of input and output goals

Next to the fact that an ambition or goal can be best formulated in output terms there are some other valuable tips for formulating engaging goals. I will illustrate them by using a real-life example at the time of writing this book.

I was working for a company that provides IT support for big companies. They had problems on different levels. Clients and employees were very frustrated about the way things were going, and the services delivered. The new General Manager was very simple and authentic in his drive and ambition, namely that their aim and main focus must be the satisfaction of the customer. All the rest would follow.

For them, a clear and engaging ambition was formulated as follows:

FROM:	TO:
80 per cent of our customers come back to complain.	Within two years our customers will be so satisfied that they testify in high-profile magazines about the enormous increase in customer satisfaction we realised in such a short period. If not, I as GM will take responsibility and resign.

Of course, if you want to make it more SMART (specific, measurable, acceptable, realistic, and time bound) then you can define which customers, in which magazines, and what they have to say. It is also wise to define a way to measure progress.

The principles used to formulate this goal were:

Formulate a Goal in Terms of 'From' and 'To'
A formulation in the 'from' and 'to' format induces movement towards your goal. It describes the current and the wanted situation and, in this way, it already makes it very clear for people what gap there is to bridge.

Use Shocking Facts to Illustrate the Current Situation
It is very useful to formulate the 'from' in terms of shocking facts. This is important because shocking facts create more engagement than vague announcements. For example, try to feel the difference between:

A. Our customer satisfaction needs to go up by 10 per cent.

B. 80 per cent of our customers give us a 5 out of 10 on customer satisfaction.

With A, people often start to think, "That's not good but, to be honest, customer satisfaction is never high enough." And, by doing this, they already start to relativize the need to act.

Option B is a fact that describes the seriousness of the situation. Here it is very hard to say that this is not a problem. Perhaps they don't see how they themselves can solve this. But all that is important right now is that they acknowledge the seriousness of the fact, which will create buy-in on the level of the problem. If you don't get buy-in on the level of the problem, there is the risk that no solution will ever be implemented. This is logical. They don't want to put energy into implementing a solution when you are not convinced that there is a problem. But we see it happening all the time.

It is important that you use the facts on an output level. They must illustrate the lack of an important possible outcome. These might include, for example, lack of client satisfaction or employee satisfaction, lack of efficiency or proficiency, the inability to grasp opportunities, or unhappiness. Using facts that point to the lack of a solution are less strong. They might include, for example, "We don't have a marketing strategy," "We don't have competence management," "There is no effective meeting structure," and so on.

Have a Cost for Not Attaining the Goal
Let's be honest. It is quite easy to formulate all kinds of thriving goals, but how real are they? How committed are you to making them happen? Putting a price on not attaining a goal increases the credibility of the goal in the eyes of your employees as well as your customers when the goal is communicated externally. For example, a supermarket in the Netherlands stated that they no longer wanted queues at the registers. As a way of keeping their promise, they said that every third client who had to wait in line would get their groceries for free. They meant what they said.

Formulate a 'To' With a Kick on an Emotional Level
Formulate the goal in a way that is not too cerebral in the numbers that you want to reach. This often implies that there will be a tap on the head when a goal is not achieved. It is much more motivating and emotionally engaging if you want to reach something awesome, something that will make people proud to work for your company. For example, if you want to deliver a high level of service to your customers, instead of defining your goal in a list of KPIs, you could formulate it as follows, "Next year, we will be mentioned as the best service provider by the biggest consumer association in our field."

However, the KPIs are still useful as a kind of dashboard to steer and to measure.

Formulate Your Own Ambition in Terms of Output Goals
Going back to the earlier example, when walking through the layers of my personality I discovered that one of my emotional needs is to get validation and approval from alphas. When exploring this further, I found that this also makes me very compassionate towards all kinds of people who aren't alphas, which can mean I'm considered the underdog within companies. I feel and recognize that these people, when led in a different way, would blossom and deliver great value. So, this is my core ambition: contributing to the development of leaders and companies by offering the same possibilities to everyone and thus creating happy, productive organisations.

So, what is the output I would like to realise within a certain amount of time? It is:

FROM:	TO:
According to Gallup, up to 70 per cent of people are not engaged in their work.	In the companies for which I am allowed to do a vast amount of work in coaching and training, we need 70 per cent of people to be engaged in their work.

Now you can go back to the ambition you formulated after walking through the layers of your personality and try to reformulate your goal in terms of 'From' and 'To.'

In the **'From'**: Use shocking facts that touch your heart.

In the **'To'**: Formulate an output and define SMART outcomes (specific, measurable, acceptable, realistic, and time bound).

How authentic, shocking facts can change the energy in the room

When facilitating a meeting of the top 50 leaders of an insurance company to co-create the future of the company, the atmosphere was stale. It felt like everyone was going through the motions, but without real passion. Nonetheless, the reason for the meeting was framed by the CEO as being super important and critical for the future of the company. He stated that the market was going through big changes; that consumer behaviour was becoming completely different; that online products and services were becoming more and more important etc. Of course, most of these things were not very new to the audience, and it did not seem to touch their hearts. At a certain moment, we decided to take the management team away separately and asked them if they shared our observations about the atmosphere within the large group of leaders. They agreed and together we concluded that they were probably going through the motions because of the framing of the meeting. It felt just like the standard talk about the world changing rapidly, blah blah blah. We asked the CEO if he had a stronger context and ambition to draw on. He immediately said, "Yes! But I cannot share it because it is sensitive information. It could hurt our stock price." After a bit more reflection with the management team, he decided to change his position and share the information he had. We took some time to prepare the shocking facts, the ambition he wanted to present from the heart, and to formulate some key boundaries to be respected when co-creating the way forward. When we went back into the conference room it suddenly became real life, with high stakes, and the energy in the room completely changed! One could feel the excitement boiling, and people immediately started organising themselves to find the right answers.

No wind blows in favour of a ship without direction.

Seneca the Younger

CHAPTER SEVEN

Setting Clear Boundaries

When an ambition is clearly defined, and people are engaged to co-create and find ways or solutions to realise this ambition, it is wise to offer clear boundaries, a canvas of guiding principles that people can autonomously work within. In my own experience, and according to author Daniel Pink, having autonomy within a clear set of boundaries is one of the most important elements in creating intrinsic motivation. It is also necessary for our emotional brain because a lack of boundaries is 'unsafe', since it's unclear which behaviour is expected and valued.

Self-exploration of your personality (from Chapter Five) is also crucial in formulating boundaries. It is important to realise that the boundaries you define can come from all kinds of true or untrue emotional needs, true or false beliefs, or from destructive parts of the ego. Again, the challenge will be to make a distinction between boundaries that are actually related to your core values and drivers (in a positive way), and those that are coming from an ego protecting your vulnerability, and not necessarily serving the interests of the ambition, or of your colleagues.

When training or coaching I start by talking about the need for boundaries, and I very often hear the remark, "Oh, but boundaries limit the creativity of people." Indeed, they do if there are too many boundaries, and when they are aimed at micromanaging people. I remember reading about an experiment in a school. The school building was in the middle of a fenced area. In the experiment, researchers wanted to know what would happen if they took away the fence. What do you think happened? When the fence was there the children used, more or less, the entire playground. When the fence was taken away, most of the children started to play closer to, and even inside, the school. People often predict that the opposite would happen; namely that children would take their freedom and explore a wider area. Some people even think that the children would take advantage of their freedom and run away. The fact that they stay closer to the school is interpreted as a need for safety. Safety that is gone when the fence is taken away.

This is easy to relate to a business context. Imagine that you get tasks from your manager, but it is not clear how the tasks correspond to the end goal, or the criteria for the work. What would happen? The risk is that you finish a task and that, after, he will say, "Oh, you spent too much money," "You took too much time," "I expected you to consult other departments," or, "I don't find it acceptable that you hired an external party." In this scenario, what your manager does is place fences when play time is finished, and then blames you for crossing them. It is the same as defining the rules of the game while playing, or even after the game is over, to decide who has won. This can cause a great deal of frustration.

It is a must, therefore, and one of the core responsibilities of a leader, to define the ambition and playing field upfront. What I see in the real world is that, when boundaries are missing, micromanagement kicks in. Without boundaries, the only way for a leader to stay in control is to be too close to the solution, which often leads to taking over the responsibilities and the freedom of the employee. The employee becomes frustrated, and is less likely to take initiative, as the risk is high that their actions will not be approved of, and they will, in turn, become passive. The latter is then a trigger for the leader to become even more involved with defining and implementing all kinds of solutions, and a vicious cycle is born. I often call this the vicious cycle of action and reaction. Leader and follower influence each other in a negative sense, over and over again, and energy, passion, and motivation go downhill.

But, as I said, having too many boundaries is as deadly as having too few. Imagine that I want to produce organic vegetables. I buy a large plot of land, which I divide among several employees, each employee getting their own piece. I have a clear ambition: I want to produce healthy organic vegetables and, of course, I will define this more concretely into goals for each employee. I will tell each of them how much I want them to produce.

I started this company because I am passionate about it. I am a walking encyclopaedia of knowledge, skill, and experience on how to cultivate organic vegetables. So, I know that you have to put the carrots close to the leeks, keep the cauliflower away from the peas, and so on. The people working for me, on their pieces of land, differ in experience: some are as experienced as me; a lot of them have less experience; some have very little skill and knowledge; and a few are more experienced than me. To ensure standardised and high production across each piece of land, I have a strong urge to put all my knowledge into the 'boundaries', in the form of rules for effective cultivation. Also, my ego will dictate all kinds of boundaries I want to impose on others in order to protect myself, to stay in maximum control, and to assure that I will be successful. Thus, my list of 'boundaries', or rules, become endless.

Not only will I tell my people how much they have to produce, but I will also tell them that:

- they cannot use chemicals.

- they get €10,000 a year to buy materials, seeds, and plants.

- the carrots have to be 40cm from the leeks.

- the cauliflower has to be at least two metres from the peas.

- they have to start planting the red cabbage before they plant strawberries.

- the paths in the garden have to be at least one metre wide.

- brussels sprouts are not permitted (and I know that there is a good market for it, with a good profit, but I don't like them).

- they have to harvest the lettuce every two weeks, on a Thursday.

I translate my knowledge into instructions, rules, and boundaries, and, in this way, I give my people the following message: you have to do it exactly like me. Things that are very positive in many respects—experience, knowledge, and skill—risk becoming a long list of rules, which for some people are a blessing, and for others are suffocating.

An exhaustive set of rules or boundaries can be a blessing for some people because it offers a lot of structure and guidance—predictability for the brain. Because there are no choices to be made, there is no risk of making mistakes. Indeed, if you have followed all the rules and the harvest is poor (perhaps because you made some other mistakes not covered in the rules), then it's easy to avoid blame. In this way, having too many boundaries can take away people's own responsibility. There is also a high chance that, if they just keep following the rules, they won't develop any autonomy, independence, or competence. So, what I am doing here is building a company filled with robots that have no passion. As soon as circumstances change—new bugs appear, there is a demand for different vegetables—and my own rules are no longer correct, I will not be able to count on the resilience of my people who never became independent, skilled gardeners, with the flexibility to adapt to new circumstances. Instead of passing on my full knowledge to help them develop, I have only given them specific rules which won't help them when things change. Intrinsic motivation will not be present and I will have to motivate them by paying bonuses. In his book, Drive: The Surprising Truth About What Motivates Us, Daniel Pink states that people feel intrinsic motivation and passion when their job offers the following aspects:

Purpose: People have to see that what they are doing serves a purpose bigger than themselves. In my garden there is such a purpose, which is cultivating healthy food, but when people are just applying prescribed rules all day long, do you think that they will feel this purpose? Purpose, as described by Daniel Pink, has the same meaning as ambition in the New Leadership ABCs. As I said earlier, it is wise to make sure that your ambitions as a leader are aligned with those of your employees. You don't achieve this just by creating rules and procedures for them to follow. It requires that employees participate in creating the vision, in decision making, and in defining the core playing field.

Mastery: Is there the possibility to get better at something? Probably the only thing the employees will get better at in my garden is following rules and procedures.

Autonomy: Is there the possibility to take initiative and to be able to influence, to a certain extent, one's own activity? I think that the story of my garden says it all!

I really don't want to create a garden or a company like this one where purpose, mastery, and autonomy are absent. What about you?

So, how to proceed? I feel that my ambition is a good one. I have a passion to cultivate organic vegetables. Perhaps I can translate it into a more engaging goal, according to the principles described in the previous chapter. Let's try.

FROM:	TO:
Studies show a relationship between the use of chemicals for growing vegetables and cancer (you can add statistics here to support this statement).	We have a mission to make sure that our food does not make people sick, so we need to produce the same amount of vegetables, with the same quality, without the use of any chemicals.

And, of course, it would not hurt to make this goal SMART and define the amount of vegetables we want to produce, as well as ensuring that we operationalize the fact that we are not using chemicals. I can also translate this main goal into specific, smaller goals for each gardener.

But now I want to define the boundaries in such a way that they guarantee my production goals, and at the same time enhance the motivation of my people as well as their skills and experiences.

An effective way to do this is to critically revise all the boundaries you want to define. The question to pose to yourself is the following:

If one of the gardeners finds a way to deliver the target production, or even more, without putting the carrots 40cm from the leeks, is that acceptable? I bet you will say yes! I certainly would. And, when I say that this is acceptable, then the rule about planting carrots 40cm from the leeks is no longer a boundary. One rule down, one hundred to go.

My advice with each rule or boundary is to ask yourself the above question. You should formulate as few boundaries as possible, while putting all of your knowledge and experience into manuals and training guides, making them available for the people who need and want them.

But perhaps an even better way forward is the other way around. Take a sheet of paper and now reflect on the following question:

For me, as a leader, which kinds of solutions, results, or behaviours*, offered by employees, are not acceptable?

Defining solutions or behaviour that are not acceptable can be done in two ways:

1. Think back to the kinds of solutions that were offered to you in the past but that, for one reason or another, you did not deem acceptable. What were these reasons? Look for situations where you were not happy with your employees' solutions, results or behaviours. For example, someone proposed a solution to you that had a negative effect for another colleague, which made things more difficult for you.

2. Think forward: If tomorrow you were to ask your employees for solutions to reach your team goals, which ones would you not accept? For example, a solution that entails leaning too much on a subcontractor, and that takes away the possibility of your employees and company acquiring skills and expertise.

*I consciously speak about solutions/results as well as about behaviours because I am convinced that both are crucial in creating a consistent set of boundaries.

As CEO of my garden, I would decline solutions and/or behaviours:

- if they are below the quality norms we have defined.

- if they don't respect the agreed upon budget.

- if someone has a poor result because of lack of knowledge and they didn't ask for help or didn't consult the manuals.

- if someone has knowledge they do not share.

- if someone has extra time that they don't use to be more productive because their work is already adequate.

- if someone picks a fight every day with one of my other gardeners.

- if someone doesn't help another employee, even if they have the ability.

- if someone tells me what is not possible, instead of what is possible.

You may have noticed that this last set of boundaries in my garden story is completely different from the first one. The first set of boundaries was a list of rules to be followed, dictated by uncertainty and defence of the ego. And, as I said earlier, rules are also often the representation of existing experience and knowledge, so there is nothing wrong with them as such. But we often see that every new incident or experience leads to a new rule or boundary, driven by a need for control. When everything is governed by rules, people will suffocate and lose their passion. The second list of boundaries is more a set of values that are very important in evaluating results delivered; they are also the way I would like employees to act and react within my company. This list is more connected to my core emotional drivers and values, as discussed in Chapter Five, where we explored the different layers of personality. By ensuring this set of boundaries is present throughout different situations—in documents and communications from me, as a leader, for example—they will form the basic culture of my company and, together with the outlined ambitions, they will become the DNA of my enterprise. To return to the garden example, imagine how much information is contained in the combination of my ambitions and the second set of boundaries.

My employees know our main goal and passion is to produce healthy vegetables. They also know the core values and boundaries of the company, within which they can develop themselves as professionals and autonomous gardeners, having fun arranging their gardens the way they see fit. The company culture is created and maintained by these boundaries, in addition to many other things. Starting from this foundation, through various channels, I can now make sure that my desired culture, based on my company DNA, will flourish. This is a truly useful way to shape company culture, and to influence and develop it according to my ambitions and my core boundaries. In Chapter Eight I will describe the shaping of company culture in more in detail, and apply it to my garden example.

Defining Your Own Set of Core Boundaries

Of course, one could define a playing field for each task or project, but it is even more valuable to reflect on the core boundaries you want people to respect when you are leading them or when others are interacting with you. In this context, it becomes a more in-depth and fundamental exercise. A lot of leaders could make their lives easier by reflecting on this, formulating a fundamental playing field, and then communicating it so that everyone knows the core boundaries and values they are working within.

A technique that helps you in defining your boundaries is to think of typical solutions, actions, or behaviours, delivered in the past by employees, that:

- are not acceptable.

- really make you angry.

- irritate you.

Here are some possible examples:

> "It disappoints me when someone from one department gives me a solution that creates a problem for another department."

> "I hate it when people come up with solutions that are not substantiated with numbers and facts."

> "I don't appreciate it when people try to reinvent the wheel without looking at what is already being done within the company."

"It is never acceptable to ignore the budget, quality standards, and safety."

"It is inefficient to avoid using the existing budget when it is available and when it would make a swift solution possible."

Translate your reactions to these solutions and behaviours into boundaries and write them down. You can formulate them in positive terms, e.g., "I expect you to always ask for help when you are struggling."

Here is an example:
"As an employee, you have autonomy to realise the company's ambitions, but we ask you to find ways to do this within the following boundaries or 'playing field':

• Respect quality, budget, and safety rules.

• Never cause problems for other departments.

• Substantiate your approach and solutions with facts and numbers, so that you can prove that it is effective and efficient and leads to the realisation of our core ambitions.

• Don't try to reinvent the wheel.

• Use the means available to you (money and people), because there is no gain in false cost savings"

Exercise: **Work on Your Own Boundaries**

Based on the material above, reflect on and write down what you consider to be your core values and principles, that form the boundaries and playing field for the people you lead.

My core values and guiding principles, to which all actions, solutions, and behaviours of the people I lead have to correspond

_____

_____

_____

_____

_____

_____

_____

_____

_____

Now, double-check your boundaries. Revise them one-by-one, and ask yourself the following question: If we have a problem and someone can offer the perfect solution, but it does not meet this particular boundary, do I still want to hear and consider it? If yes, eliminate or revise this boundary.

For example: You have a serious problem in department X and someone offers you a good solution, but this would have a negative effect on department Y. Would you consider it, or not? If yes, then you have to rephrase this boundary or eliminate it.

As for the remaining boundaries, try to make them as clear and specific as possible.

For example, "I expect you to work together," is perhaps too general because working together can mean several things. You can make this more specific by saying, "When you need help, ask for it. I will not accept a bad result when you did not ask for help." And, "When you learn something, share it with the rest of us. I want to regularly hear and see you sharing with others."

If needed, rewrite them:

Revised: My core values and guiding principles, to which all actions, solutions, and behaviours of the people I lead have to correspond

_____

_____

_____

_____

_____

_____

_____

_____

_____

_____

CASE STUDY SEVEN:

An oil refinery in distress because of a lack of boundaries

I was recently in contact with Maria, an HR manager, who consulted with me to develop the leadership at an oil refinery. The main issue they were having seemed to be the fact that absenteeism had been high for several years, but had gotten particularly bad over the last year. She told me that employees had not seemed very happy for several years, and that they had lost faith in the future of the plant. They saw their factory as old and without much investment from the owners. However, the facts seemed to contradict this. Although the amount invested was not enormous (because the people didn't seem to be highly motivated), there were no factual indications that there was no future for the plant.

When I had the first two-day session with the management team, to define a plan to turn this situation around, the team felt like a mess. People were absent, late, and leaving the sessions to have online meetings. They were constantly discussing anecdotes that weren't relevant. When we addressed this, they acknowledged it, and promised that they would act differently.

Over the years, the team had developed a culture of having no boundaries and not respecting the few they had. The company's analysis was that middle management was not skilled and mature enough to handle absenteeism and lack of motivation. However, when we organised a one-day session with middle management and employees, to facilitate a dialogue on how to tackle this problem, it appeared that middle management was little involved or consulted on anything. And, although the day brought middle management and the employees closer together, it did not lead to fundamental change. The employees still lacked boundaries and discipline, which radiated to the rest of the company, creating a hectic atmosphere. This was the fundamental problem. Employees without boundaries or meaning led to:

- long meetings with few results.
- no clear decisions.
- no clear communication about the future of the plant.
- no defined boundaries for middle managers (and they, in turn, were unable to give boundaries and structure to their employees).

CHAPTER EIGHT

Culture and Coaching

What is Culture and Why is it So Important?

At this point in the book, you, as a leader, have defined a core ambition and a set of boundaries that contain your core values. In the previous chapter, I discussed how your boundaries, if well defined, could be the basis of your team or company culture.

But the definition of culture needs more attention. Culture can be defined as the way things are done within your team or company and how people interact with each other. At the core of culture, there is always a paradigm reflecting core beliefs and assumptions on how the world and people function. Very often, these are the beliefs and assumptions of those who started the company, or those who currently have a strong influence. For example, if the founders of the company had a vision that everything needed to be planned and controlled to make things happen, then it is likely that this became the leading paradigm for the organisation, with a lot of structure, procedures, and control as a consequence. Ambitions and boundaries are, in my opinion, a good place to start in terms of influencing the culture of an organisation.

I remember reading the striking phrase, "The invisible gap between plan and realisation is... culture."

Indeed, many detailed plans are made to realise change within companies, but about 70 per cent of these fail, primarily because of the culture. Making a plan is one thing, but getting people engaged is a completely different ballgame. I strongly believe that, in contemporary and future organisations, the culture will be the determining factor for success. Because our world is changing rapidly, adaptability will be key going forward. Employees need flexibility, so they can adapt and react to different circumstances without violating the core boundaries and 'emotional impact' of the company. The emotional impact of a company is the way the company makes you feel, as a customer. If you want to steer the behaviour of individuals, teams, departments, or even of the entire company by control (e.g. systems, procedures, and many rules), then it is likely impossible to obtain the adaptability you need. I see the New Leadership ABCs as a more effective way to lead a company. By defining ambitions, the playing field (boundaries), and building a culture that develops and coaches people to handle their autonomy in the right way, you can build a flexible company. I believe the aim of leading a company, or a team, is to make sure that its value for the internal or external customer is consistent and impactful on an emotional level. Apple is a good example. In each one of their products I can feel the good taste and the love for beautifully-designed objects that give you that feeling of being part of the future and belonging to a larger club of like-minded people. This is what I call the emotional impact of a product, service, or of an organisation. You achieve this impact, not through control, but by building the right culture in a solid way.

Fostering Organisational Culture

To foster the culture you want, you, as a leader, can make all the difference. How? Next to defining engaging ambitions and creating a clear playing field, the concept of the Cultural Web, developed by Gerry Johnson and Kevan Scholes, is a very interesting tool to use. It gives you the right buttons to push, in order to influence your culture in the right direction.

Here are their descriptions of the different elements an organisation can use to make the invisible culture tangible and visible. Together, they reflect the fundamental paradigm leading the company's actions.

1. **Stories:** The past events and people talked about, inside and outside the company. Who and what the company chooses to immortalize says a great deal about what it values and perceives as great behaviour.

2. **Rituals and Routines:** The daily behaviour and actions of people, that signal acceptable behaviour. This determines what is expected to happen in given situations, and what is valued by management.

3. **Symbols:** The visual representations of the company, including logos, how plush the offices are, and the formal or informal dress codes.

4. **Organisational Structure:** This includes both the structure defined by the organisation chart, and the unwritten lines of power and influence that indicate whose contributions are most valued.

5. **Control Systems:** The ways that the organisation is controlled. These include financial systems, quality systems, and rewards (including the way they are measured and distributed within the organisation).

6. **Power Structures:** The pockets of real power in the company. This may involve one or two key senior executives, a whole group of executives, or even a department. The key is that these people have the greatest amount of influence on decisions, operations, and strategic direction.

Let me reuse my garden example from Chapter Seven. The two sets of boundaries that I defined were very different in nature. The first was aimed at leading my organic garden in a rather strict and regulated way, with a lot of boundaries and rules. The second only has a few rules that are more value-driven and focused on how interactions within my garden should take place. Both sets of boundaries will need very different elements, as described by the Cultural Web. The table below outlines the differences, using this tool, between the old garden with all of its rules and regulations, and the new garden with only core boundaries and values.

Paradigm one: The old garden with all of its rules and regulations	Paradigm two: The new garden with only core boundaries and values
Control systems:	**Control systems:**
I would need a very elaborate system of control. Indeed, I would have to be able to ensure that the carrots are exactly at 40cm from the leeks, that the cauliflower is at least two metres from the peas, that the red cabbage is planted before planting the strawberries, etc.	I am going to observe and measure if people respect behaviours i.e. quality norms, if they share, if they look for help, if they help others, etc.
Power:	**Power:**
The power would be entirely in my hands. I would regularly make new rules and follow them through.	I have to be consistent and not meddle with the autonomy of my gardeners. I need to exhibit behaviour that shows that I have the power to formulate ambitions and boundaries and to follow up on these, but that their power is not threatened in their own gardens.
Structure:	**Structure:**
Because so much control is needed, I would create a more layered organisation. I would have team managers that could control a group of gardeners.	All gardeners will be reporting directly to me, stressing their autonomy.
Symbols:	**Symbols:**
I would place my office in the middle of the garden, so that my team managers can talk to me directly. They would be in a circle around me, and between the gardeners and myself.	I will place my office at the border of the garden, to show that I am looking at the whole enterprise but that I don't form its centre. This will emphasize the fact that the employees have to interact with each other directly and not through me. I will have to find a new logo, for customers as well as for employees, that illustrates the ambitions and values we cherish.

Paradigm one: The old garden with all of its rules and regulations	Paradigm two: The new garden with only core boundaries and values
Routines and rituals:	Routines and rituals:
I will introduce monthly meetings where experiences are shared on how to apply the rules more effectively, and not on how to get better results.	I will encourage every gardener to say hello to their neighbours through my own behaviour. I will introduce a monthly meeting, just to share experience and knowledge. Every year we will all go together to the national conference for biological cultivation.
Stories:	Stories:
I have to make heroes out of the people that respect my boundaries i.e. the people who make sure that carrots are exactly 40cm from the leeks. Those people and their stories will become topic of the day.	I have to make heroes out of the people that respect my boundaries. The people who share, seek help, and respect quality will be put in the spotlight and their stories will be told. These will generate a company mythology that incorporates my boundaries and ambitions.

Figure 8.1 Fostering organisational culture using the Cultural Web

Depending on your position, and the influence you have within the company, you can help to define all of these components. You can define the structure, the power, and the control systems, and you can influence who will be the heroes, what the symbols will be, which routines and rituals become important, and which stories will become the anecdotes discussed at the coffee machine, in meetings, and at parties. The main way to do this is to use your attention and appreciation wisely. The things you give attention and appreciation will flourish.

Last but not least, it is your role to make sure that people and teams are able to do their jobs and also grow as people and professionals. Of course, all people are different, and some have a lot of experience, while others are just beginning. Some are well motivated, while others need a small push or pull to become motivated. Some are experienced and already motivated, but there is almost always a difficult moment where they will need your help. Some don't use their initiative in a way that corresponds with your ambitions and the boundaries you defined. They will need some kind of coaching, or even a correction.

Setting an Example with Your Behaviour

Coaching will make sure that people master the skills they need to become the type of employee that can act, independently and wisely, when confronted with unexpected changes or questions.

Now I want to focus on some core concepts that will help you to do what is really necessary when coaching people, namely, to be a living example of the culture you desire and the boundaries you have defined. Perhaps this will sound a bit strange, but there is often quite a difference between wanting a particular culture and enacting this culture on an individual, team, or organisational level. I often see that organisations and leaders want or desire self-starting, wise employees, but then create an environment that promotes the opposite. For example, leaders are too active themselves and, without even realising it, they give all the solutions and answers to employees. The consequence is that employees become passive and don't develop into the type of employee that the leader wants.

Leaders should be consistent in verbal behaviour (the ambition and boundaries you translate through words) and non-verbal behaviour (the behaviour you show and the way in which you communicate). If you say, "I want you to be active," but in your own behaviour you are so active that there is almost no opportunity for others to do so, then only your behaviour will have an impact, not your words!

This is essential. Every day I hear leaders, at all levels, verbalise vision, values, and ideas that are intended to motivate and develop people, but at the same time the behaviour they show gives a completely different message. It is their behaviour that forms the real message, which will determine if ideas and vision become reality—or not.

As discussed earlier, the reason for this is that a leader's non-verbal behaviour communicates directly with the limbic brain of their employees, the part of the brain where behaviour is initiated. Their words only communicate to the employees' rational brains, and therefore don't always have the power to convince the limbic brain to initiate behaviour. I am convinced that, as long as the limbic brain has a bad feeling, nothing will happen besides fighting against the message (and perhaps the messenger) by freezing, or fleeing. To some extent, you can influence a feeling with words, but it's much more effective to influence it with your non-verbal behaviour.

Exercise: **Defining Your Desired Culture**

Part one: Use the table below to think about the different elements of the Cultural Web and how they show themselves within your team, department and/or organisation. Then think about how you would like to change them. Write down possible ideas you have to make this move 'from'...'to.'

Make sure you do part one before you even look at part two of this exercise

CULTURAL WEB ELEMENTS	HOW IT IS NOW From...	HOW I WANT IT To...	IDEAS TO CHANGE IT
Structure			
Power			
Control systems			
Symbols			
Routines and rituals			
Stories			

Part two: Now review how you would like to change the different elements of the Cultural Web. Look at all the suggestions together, and discover the core of the change you want. What is the paradigm shift you are targeting?

Coaching: **Where to Focus when Coaching and Developing People**

When developing and coaching people, or guiding them through a change process, I always follow the principle that people will be engaged and take ownership when the following four elements are fulfilled:

1. Awareness. People have to be aware of what is expected from them. They must also realise the importance of these expectations. And this is not as simple as it sounds! During one of my first times coaching there was a situation in which a leader had been asking an employee, year after year, to write a vision for the future for IT. The team member he was asking was experienced, and the leader estimated that he should be easily capable of doing this. The frustration was growing; this employee always said he would write the report, but he never did. After talking with the employee and the leader, it became painfully clear that they had completely different expectations of what a vision on IT was. The leader was frustrated because he knew the employee had so much experience and insight, and that he could likely write the report in half a day, without blinking. The employee, who had a completely different personality than the leader, felt that this report would require him to study, read books, form a project group, and involve other people to get this done. Once the expectations were clear, the vision was swiftly delivered. People often think that they understand each other and that mutual expectations are clear.

    The other element of awareness is that people need to know the importance of what is expected of them. In this example, it had to be clear why the employee's vision of the future of IT was needed, and why it was so important. If a leader cannot give at least two clear facts about why an output is needed, it can't be that important!

2. Willingness. Once people are aware of what is expected, they need to be willing to do what is asked of them. There can be different reasons why they are not willing. The first may be that awareness is not yet 100 per cent. In that sense, awareness is the basis for all other elements. Perhaps the employees don't agree with what you are asking of them, even if they are aware of what you want, and how important it is. They might think, "This is not for me," "I don't like this," "I don't see myself doing this," etc. Or, people can have all kinds of emotions and beliefs that block them from moving in the direction you would like them to go, even if they are inspired to do it. And, of course, sometimes these feelings and beliefs are valid! For

example, an employee can be aware of and see the absolute need to become more customer-focused, but can realistically conclude that this work will require behaviour and skills that they don't feel comfortable with. In that case, it is wise to look for another solution. When employees are afraid that they are not capable of the desired behaviour, one of the main reasons they get stuck is a lack of willingness to express this to their leader. A very common belief people have is that, if their leader asks them to do something, they feel that they must be capable of doing it, and then they get stuck in a place of doubt and inactivity. If you don't have the sensitivity as a leader to see this, and talk about it, you will perceive it as being resistance and unwillingness to do the work.

In the case of the employee who was expected to write the IT report, he saw it as being something so big that he could never find the time to realise it. Once he knew that his leader saw it as something much simpler, and just expected him to write it from his own experience, he still felt resistance in the sense of, "Will this be good enough? How serious will anyone take a vision of IT written by one person?" Even with a better understanding of what was required, it still took a few additional discussions with his leader and me to explore his beliefs and feelings, to support him, and to solve his concerns. Once he was listened to, and had support to solve his concerns, he was fully engaged and motivated to do the job.

3. Ability. Being aware and willing does not mean that people have the skills and knowledge to act as needed. It is important to foresee the necessary training, coaching, and peer group developments that might be needed to make sure people are supported and get the necessary skills and knowledge. In the case of the employee working in IT, he was well skilled in IT and in predicting the future, but had poor writing skills. So, he was matched to a colleague who was very skilled at writing.

4. Courage. This is often the most difficult element to tackle. People can be fully aware, willing, and able, but can't find the final courage to act. They are often afraid to look silly or fail. In the case of the employee working in IT, he needed some support every once in a while, in the form of talks with his leader, as reassurance that what he was doing was good enough and that he was on the right track.

In the table below I describe what you, as a leader and coach, can do to tackle these four elements, which can get in the way of people moving in the desired direction.

Exercise: **What do Your People Need to Grow?**

List your direct reports and make a short assessment on how they are doing, at this moment, in the areas of awareness, willingness, ability and courage. No need to write something for each aspect of each direct report. Just assess what is most important for that person and use some key words. Then look in the table below (Figure 8.2) for possible actions.

Direct report	Awareness	Willingness	Ability	Courage	Possible actions or ideas

HOW TO IMPROVE AWARENESS

- Give facts, numbers, and examples to show the need for a change or a certain (different) behaviour.

- Don't be vague.

- Tell it as it is, but with respect for people.

- Don't blame, but be factual and descriptive.

- Make sure that you awake the crocodile brain, but you don't put it into fight, freeze or flight modes (see later chapters on communication and interaction).

- Ask a lot of questions! Do they see the need for change? Why? Why not?

- Disconnect 'being aware' from 'being able to solve a challenge.' People's emotional brain often refuses to become aware because it does not see a way to solve the problem, so it goes into denial. You can say, "You don't have to see a solution, I just want to make sure you see the problem."

HOW TO IMPROVE WILLINGNESS

- Listen, ask questions, ask more questions, observe non-verbal behaviour, explore and put yourself in the other person's shoes. All of this is to discover the beliefs and feelings that are blocking people, and to give support wherever possible to overcome concerns.

- Don't be tempted to reassure people without knowing what exactly is bothering them, e.g., "Don't be worried," "Everything will be OK,", "Look at it in a more optimistic way," "See it as an opportunity," etc. Often these are perceived as hollow phrases that don't fully explore the other person's concerns.

HOW TO IMPROVE ABILITY	• Define which skills and knowledge are necessary, and involve people to determine them. • Find ways to provide development by connecting people, organising training (online and real world), having regular talks and short instructive meetings, and instituting peer coaching.
HOW TO IMPROVE COURAGE	• Listen and support people. • Stress your belief in them. Be factual and descriptive about why you believe in them, again avoiding hollow phrases. • Give them honest compliments. • Reward courage by giving it attention. • Offer them low-risk situations in which to practice. • Defend them and take the blame yourself if they make a mistake.

Figure 8.2 Improving the four key elements that will engage and develop your employees

In my experience, these four elements are very effective as a diagnostic tool (why are things not moving?) and a coaching/development tool (what can we do to make it move?) However, for coaching and development to be effective, there needs to be openness and safety within the relationship between employees and leaders, and within teams and among employees. That is why core communication and interaction skills are fundamental to putting all of this into practice. These skills will determine if people will open up and be honest about their expectations, desires, and concerns. Without this, a whole organisation can be role-playing and paying 'lip service' to this process, where they say that everything is going well and that everyone is on board, without this really being the case. This is one of the core reasons why a company might not be swinging towards success.

In the next chapters, I will be describing a few core insights and tools to boost your interaction and communication style and behaviour as a leader, as well as that of your team or company. First, I will explain the fundamentals of all communication, namely the fact

that in each communication, in each sentence you speak, even
in each facial expression, that there are always several different
messages present on different levels. Second, I will explain and
describe the core dynamics of building social relationships that create
energy, motivation, and personal and professional development.
It is absolutely fundamental to make sure that your ambition and
boundaries are communicated clearly, and that people are developing
the ability to build a happy, productive, and winning company.

How culture can and needs to shift when core paradigms shift

Company culture is fascinating. When working for a large retail company, I experienced how each company culture has a kind of central paradigm on which it is based. Each has its own core beliefs on how things work and how things should be done. This retail company had one store that was also an example and training centre for other stores worldwide. But something did not feel right. The people running the store often complained that some of their employees were constantly travelling to share knowledge and expertise, and that this was at the expense of the store itself. When the employees were travelling, they were not available to help the store progress, which was affecting its results. It felt to me like they had two business models and company cultures that were competing with each other, delivering confusion and undermining the desired results.

We had everyone enter a process where they used the Cultural Web to analyse their culture and its central paradigm. By analysing their organisational structure, the distribution of power, their control and measuring systems, their routines and rituals, the stories told, their heroes, and their symbols, they discovered what was at the core of their thinking and feeling, and therefore at the core of their culture. They believed their paradigm was that they were like every other store and needed to function that way. Although they always acted according to this paradigm, once they saw it written in black and white, they realised that it was not true! They were not like every other store. Reflecting on this, they realised that they had more impact worldwide being a training and expertise centre. The results, satisfaction, and added value they built for the company was many times higher being a centre of expertise than that of being a store. This was also the case for the employees who were working in the store and not travelling and educating, as they could be seen as the ones creating the expertise.

They decided to make this the core of their paradigm and everything changed. Everyone realised that they were a training and expertise centre, and, as a result, the stories, symbols, structure, control systems, and heroes all started to change, stimulated by the leadership of the store.

Once they determined their core paradigm, we began coaching. Some of the main topics we covered were:

- Were people fully aware of the importance and need for this shift?

- Were they willing to go along with this change in perspective?

- Did they have the right knowledge and skills to fully embrace the new paradigm?

- Did they have the courage to make the necessary changes?

PART IV

Coaching and Culture in More Detail: Core Concepts, Dynamics, and Tools

CHAPTER NINE

The Foundation: Levels of Communication

In this chapter, I cover some of the core principles of human communication and what makes it either effective or ineffective. Taking these principles into account will ensure that we respect the SCARF elements discussed in Chapter Four. In this way, we will be able to communicate in a rational way and avoid putting the emotional brain into fight, flight, or freeze mode. It is the limbic system that will finally decide if people will act upon your words in a positive or negative way.

Communication is more about relation than content

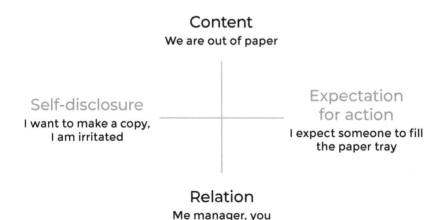

Content
We are out of paper

Self-disclosure
I want to make a copy,
I am irritated

Expectation
for action
I expect someone to fill
the paper tray

Relation
Me manager, you
assistant

Figure 9.1 The fundamentals of all communication and interaction

Communication is not only about content and the words you speak. Whenever you say something, you communicate on four levels, namely:

1. **The content level:** This is the neutral and exact meaning of the words you speak.

2. **The self-disclosure level:** Whenever you say something, you disclose something about yourself, often without knowing or realising it.

3. **The expectation for action level:** Most words and sentences we speak maintain a call for action, in one way or another.

4. **The relationship level:** Most of the things you say to someone also have a hidden message on how you see your relationship with that person.

Take the following very simple situation as an example. You are a manager and you want to make a photocopy, so you go to the copier, which is very close to the desk of the assistant to a manager. When you arrive at the copier, you see that there is no paper in the tray and you say, "Oh, we're out of paper."

This simple sentence is the content. But, by saying this, you tell others something about yourself. In this example, you are saying that you want to make a photocopy and, perhaps, depending on your tone of voice, that you are irritated that there is no paper in the tray.
This is what we call the self-disclosure level. When you speak to people, they often unconsciously pick up a lot of information about you as a person. In this scenario they may pick up that you are easily irritated, or that you expect other people to fill the paper tray.

The next level is the expectation for action level. Included in many of the things we say are requests for action. A request for action can be communicated explicitly, in which case you might say, "Can you please fill the paper tray?", or more implicitly, "We are out of paper." It is possible that you intend this as a request for action, or you might just be expressing your observation. However, people nearby can, and often will, hear it as a call for action. On the other hand, if you do intend it as a call for action, sometimes people may not hear it that way. But, if the manager's assistant is nearby, they will probably hear it as a call for action, as they probably see this as part of their role.

The last of the four levels is the relationship level, in which every word you say to someone defines your relationship with that person.

Intended or not, if the manager's assistant hears what you say as a call for action, it is as a message about how you see your relationship—you as a manager, he or she as an assistant.

Here we can link the four communication levels with the elements of SCARF. Often, on this relationship level, you will violate one of the SCARF elements: the status of the other, their autonomy, their relatedness with you, the fairness of what you are saying, and so on. We are not usually conscious of this. This means that communication, on an emotional level, can cause a disturbance, which is often not intended. This can lead to a freeze, fight, or flight response and, from that moment on, a rational discussion becomes difficult. Conflicts and discussion are often not about the content of the talk, but about the fact that, at a relational level, disrespect is communicated or perceived.

Another crucial thing to understand is that all of this is very subjective and subject to interpretation.

Figure 9.2 visualizes the other elements that come into play, namely the fact that in communication there is always an 'inside', an 'outside', and the 'other side.'

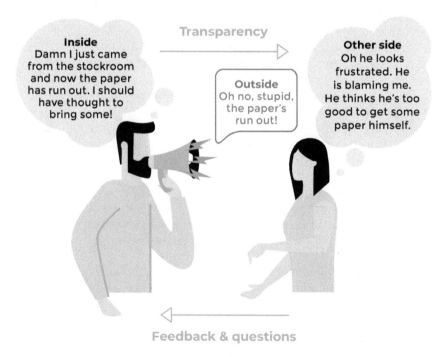

Figure 9.2 The subjectivity of communication

Inside: This is your intention, what you are thinking, and what you want to express. In this example, the person is blaming himself for something; he was in the stockroom and forgot paper.

Outside: This is the way you formulate things and the words you use, together with non-verbal behaviour, e.g. tone of voice, body posture, facial expressions, etc. In Figure 9.2, by adding the word "stupid," and by using an irritated tone of voice, the speaker adds emotion to his communication. By using the word "stupid," there is a higher risk that someone will take offence.

You are undoubtedly noticing the big difference between what is being thought (self-blame), and the words spoken (which can be perceived as blaming the manager's assistant).

Other side: Your conversation partner will always make an interpretation of what you are saying and showing (non-verbally). Depending on the sensitivity and the background of the other person, a sentence can trigger positive or negative connotations. In Figure 9.2, you see that the latter is the case. The risk of upsetting people is substantial because our brains are sensitive to status, certainty, autonomy, relatedness, and fairness (SCARF). Our brains are always listening for information about our status in reference to other people: "Do I have to defend status, certainty, autonomy, relatedness, and fairness, or is it respected?" To assess this, our emotional brain is always listening 'between the lines' without us being conscious of it.

There is a lot within communication that is subjective, and depends on many different elements. Does this mean that you cannot manage your communication effectively? On the contrary. There are two key mechanisms for managing perceptions within a conversation, either with a team, or with an individual:

1. **Transparency.** Be as transparent as you can be. Be as specific as possible in translating your thoughts and intents into words, and don't give space for misinterpretation. This is especially important when you feel that there is some pressure or strain on the relationship.

   In the example given in Figure 9.2, if the man had said, "Oh no, how stupid of me," it would have made all the difference in the world.

2. **Feedback and questions.** If you are on the other side, give feedback on how you interpret what the other person is doing or saying. In Figure 9.2, the assistant could say, "The fact that you are saying that you've run out of paper in an angry voice gives me the

impression that you are blaming me. Is this so?" Or simply, "Are you talking or referring to me?"

By doing this, you will help to avoid misunderstandings and misinterpretations. Also, as I will explain later in more detail, a very effective intervention is posing a question, to clarify what the other person is saying and to make sure that you don't interpret something incorrectly. The assistant could ask the simplest question possible, "What is going on?"

Together, all parties in a conversation can make sure that the real intention of communication comes across, and that the crocodile or emotional limbic brain does not feel attacked by a violation of the SCARF elements.

Does this mean that we always have to be very careful and gentle when we speak? Absolutely not—being too careful and gentle also violates the SCARF principles. If you are too soft or careful you risk people treating you like a child, which is a clear violation of the status principle. Instead, you should:

1. **Give transparency:** If there is any possibility that the other person will misinterpret your communication, then make sure that you include the intent of it. Explain why you are saying what you are saying.

2. **Be factual and specific:** This is one of the golden rules in communication. Don't speak in terms of judgements, labels, or evaluations, but state the facts, the numbers and examples. Then you can add why you want it to change, "For me this is unacceptable, not realistic; hurtful, not effective." This is also the way to give effective feedback. Start by giving the facts or describing the behaviour in a neutral way, then add how it affects you.

Figure 9.3 The essential components of specific communication

Here are some examples:

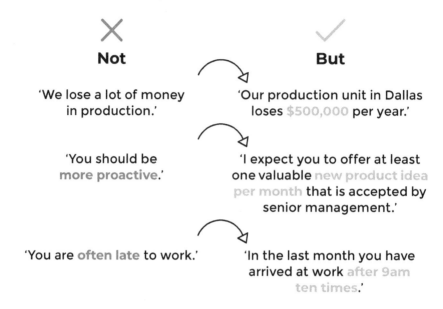

Not	But
'We lose a lot of money in production.'	'Our production unit in Dallas loses $500,000 per year.'
'You should be more proactive.'	'I expect you to offer at least one valuable new product idea per month that is accepted by senior management.'
'You are often late to work.'	'In the last month you have arrived at work after 9am ten times.'

Figure 9.4 Examples of specific feedback

So, when giving feedback in an effective way it would sound as follows:

Description of behaviour: "When I am telling you something, I notice that, before I end a sentence, you are already asking a question."

How the behaviour affects me: "I feel thrown off track and I notice that I get irritated when it happens more than once."

If you trust the leader you trust the message.

63%

of co-workers don't trust their leader

(Forbes)

So, this is the way communication and interaction works? Then I'll do it just like that!

Christophe was, and still is, a brilliant engineer working for the research and development department of one of the largest electronics companies in the world. He was valued by his boss for his creative thinking and problem-solving skills. However, Christophe did not make a lot of friends within his company. Whenever he was working with colleagues from his own department or from others, eventually there was trouble. Christophe functioned in a completely rational way: he stated the facts as he saw them, he talked to people only when he needed to gather facts, and he did not inform or consult others. Christophe stated his opinions in a brutally direct way. Because of this, others often had the feeling that he had contempt for them. He did not realise that, when communicating, it is not only about the rational facts but also about other more relational and emotional nuances. This was especially true and important because of the culture of the company. His boss finally reached the point where he had to take action. He said Christophe either had to change or it was time to say goodbye, despite his enormous expertise and problem-solving capacities. The relational cost to the company was just too big.

The main problem was that Christophe did not know that, next to straightforward content i.e. numbers and facts, communication is even more about:

- What you tell people about yourself (In the eyes of others, Christophe was always saying that he knew better and could resolve everything on his own).

- What you expect from others (Christophe implicitly gave the message, "Don't meddle, let me do my work, keep quiet and accept what I am doing.")

- How you define the relationship (Between the lines, Christophe was saying, "I am cleverer than you, you are in an operational role, which is less important than R&D.")

But this story has a rather surprising and even funny twist.
After building a relationship with Christophe, I told him in a very
straightforward way how I saw his communication and interactions
with others and why I thought it would never work. He looked at
me very surprised and said, "Is this the way it works? OK, then I
will do things differently." From a rational perspective, he could
understand what I was saying, and he suddenly understood
what had been happening. From then on, he started to change.
In additional coaching sessions he was very eager to learn,
to get feedback, and to understand the psychological side of
communication and interaction.

CHAPTER TEN

The Leadership Compass

The Main Dynamics of Interaction and Influence: Action and Reaction

In this chapter, I will introduce the main tool that can help you to manage and build interactions. It will enable you to stimulate people to develop, and become independent and engaged employees, who act and react flexibly and proactively based on the company's DNA— its purpose and boundaries. This tool will also help you approach different kinds of people in different ways, a basic necessity for leading and coaching.

The concept I use is based on Leary's Rose, which was developed by the psychologist Timothy Leary. However, I have adapted it on the basis of my own experience in leadership development and insights from brain research. I now call it the Leadership Compass. For the original hate/love axe, often referred to as the against/together dimension, I use I/We (see below). This is more in correspondence with the tendencies of our emotional brain. In this way the concept gets a new value as it represents the tensions caused by the mammal/ emotional brain that arose when humans started to live in group. The dominance dimension (see below) represents the need to find a good place in the pecking order and the I/We axe reflects the struggle between the two ways in which this can be done, namely: getting ahead by defending own interests (I) or getting ahead by getting along by striving for win-win (We). Furthermore I simplified the concept in such a way that it is easy to use in daily practice.

The leadership compass is about behaviour, and specifically how one behaviour triggers another. This triggering occurs according to predictable patterns and laws. So, if you know the patterns, then you know which behaviour you can show (verbally and non-verbally), to react effectively to the behaviour of an employee, colleague, manager, partner, child, and so on.

Reacting effectively means exhibiting behaviour that encourages the conversation to evolve into a dialogue, where everybody is discussing things as mature people, looking for the best ideas and solutions.

The Concepts of Action and Reaction

From the moment people begin to interact, their verbal and non-verbal behaviour can be categorised according to two dimensions:

Active

The first is called the 'dominance dimension,' with active behaviour on one side, and passive behaviour on the other.

With active behaviour, we mainly mean behaviour that displays the initiative to organise, to lead, to determine what is going to happen, and to formulate the agenda for a conversation.

Active behaviour can be seen more as dominant or steering rather than 'doing a lot,' as one can be very active in terms of doing all kinds of things, without leading or being dominant.

Passive behaviour means taking little or no initiative to influence an interaction or a situation. It's keeping quiet, following, obediently executing tasks, or sometimes resisting in a silent and passive way.

It's in this first dimension that we also find the first law or predictable pattern. Research shows that active behaviour triggers passive behaviour, and vice versa. This means that, when you take a lot of initiative, you dial down the initiative of others.

On the other hand, if you take very little initiative, you push or stimulate others to take more.

As a leader, this is crucial. You probably became a leader because you have a lot of initiating power. And, roughly speaking, your employees are probably not leaders because they have less initiating power (of course, this will be very different for different employees). So, there is the risk that, if you take too much initiative yourself, others may become more passive.

However, the more passive they become, the more active and initiating you will be, and this often becomes a vicious cycle. This often starts unconsciously and leads to great frustration, both with the leader and the employees.

Passive

Leaders often say that employees don't take the initiative that they should, and the employees often think (although they don't often say it out loud) that they are not allowed to act on their own initiative, or that they never get the opportunity to do so.

I ——————————————————————— We

Now, let's have a look at the second dimension. This is the "I" and "we" dimension. On the "I" side, you are mainly defending your own interests, ideas, solutions and convictions. That means that the behaviour you display communicates your own ideas and interests, or, if you are more passive, you keep quiet, disagree, and have your own ideas but don't express them. You are sending the messagethat you are only interested in your own perspective, either actively or passively.

On the "we" side, you also have your own ideas, but others can see and feel that you want to work together. You demonstrate that you are also interested in them, that you want to take their feelings into account and, if remotely possible, their ideas and interests. But, remember that the other person has to see this in your non-verbal and verbal behaviour. Having the intention and willingness to work with other people is not enough, you have to make this intention visible and clear in what you say and do. The sort of behaviour to show should include the following: asking questions, listening, acknowledging, and speaking in terms of facts, numbers and examples (as we discussed in Chapter Nine).

So, in the active "we" modus, you are putting your ideas on the table but, at the same time, you are exploring the thoughts of the other person; in the end, you will be talking about how both your and their ideas can be integrated into a win-win for both parties.

In the passive "we" modus, you are happy to accept, follow, and execute the ideas of the other.

In this second dimension of "I" and "we," we find two laws or predictable patterns. Research shows that "I" behaviour triggers "I" behaviour. If you defend your agenda, others will do the same. In this case, you often end up in a black-or-white argument until one side backs down, frustrated because they feel they have to 'give in'.

Similarly, "we" behaviour triggers "we" behaviour. If you start off by going for a win-win, you will notice that this will stimulate the other to do the same. Here you have a big opportunity to end the interaction with a win-win agreement. Also possible is a situation in which one party is following, but with pleasure, because they want to follow. This is quite different from backing down or giving in, which is the effect you get with "I" behaviour.

In summary, there are three laws predicting how your behaviour will influence the behaviour of others, and vice versa:

- **Active triggers passive, and vice versa:** You showing active behaviour will stimulate others to show passive behaviour, and others being passive will trigger you to become active.

- **"We" triggers "we":** You listening to and respecting others will trigger the same behaviour in them.

- **"I" triggers "I":** You defending your own perspective and interests will stimulate others to do the same.

This translates to four possible positions people can take in an interaction, be it face-to-face or in a group, that make up the four behaviour types in the Leadership Compass. Before I describe them, first let me talk about an important aspect of this concept, namely: We are talking about behaviour and not personality.

Personality or Behaviour?

Behaviour is related to your personality, but that doesn't mean that you can't learn to behave in a different way than it dictates. While personality isn't always visible, behaviour means the things you say and do, together with your non-verbal expressions, such as tone of voice, rhythm of speaking, posture, and facial expressions.

Here are some examples to clarify what I mean, and how it can work:

Example one: You might be a very introverted and timid (personality), but you can learn how to speak up, how to present ideas within a group, and how to raise your hand and ask questions. Based on your personality, you might naturally take a more passive and following role, but you can learn to demonstrate more active behaviour.

Example two: Your personality is very dominant and competitive. However, that does not mean that you can't learn how to listen to people, and how to explore their perspectives and needs.

In essence, your personality will define a preference for certain behaviours, but you can develop yourself and learn how to use all kinds of behaviours, be they active, passive, "I," or "we." Your personality does not have to change—although, as I described earlier, it can or will in the long run, when you change your behaviour.

Showing active, passive, "I," or "we" behaviour is something that will not only change from situation to situation, but also from phrase to phrase.

Here is an example of a conversation between a leader and a worker, about the fact that the worker should take more initiative:

Role	Sentence	Explanation	Alternative	Explanation
Leader	"Hi Joe, I want to talk again about the fact that you should take more initiative."	This is "I" / active behaviour. The leader is blunt and only speaks from his own perspective and in a judgmental way. The emotional brain will go to fight, flight, or freeze mode.	"Hi Joe, welcome. I would like to discuss with you the following, in order to find a solution. Yesterday, during the meeting, we discussed your project and I noticed that you were not saying anything about it."	This includes a lot of words that show that Joe is important to the leader. It is also more factual and doesn't label Joe.
Worker	"Yes, but I don't understand the problem."	Because of the "I" / active behaviour, the worker goes on the defensive.	"Oh, what do you mean?"	Here, the worker shows interest in the leader's perspective.

Figure 10.1 An example of active, "I" phrasing, compared to active, "we" phrasing

What should be clear from this, is that almost every sentence you speak, and every look you give, can steer a discussion or a meeting in totally different directions. It often determines if the discussion becomes a debate, a fight, or a dialogue. It is up to you to choose what you want, and to use the right verbal and non-verbal behaviour accordingly.

The Four Behaviour Types within the Leadership Compass

I have labelled the four areas with their own colour, so I will be talking about yellow, green, blue, and red behaviour (not yellow, green, blue, or red personality types).

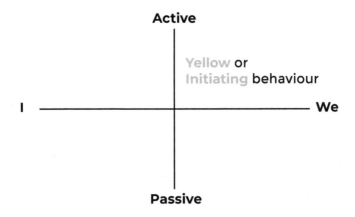

Figure 10.2 Positive initiating behaviour (yellow)

The right, upper corner is the combination of active and "we." This I call yellow behaviour (the colour of the kings), or positive initiating behaviour. You have a strong opinion, you take the initiative to formulate what you think and want, you propose action or solutions, you organise and coordinate, but always while showing that other people are important to you. This showing consists of asking questions, listening and exploring the wishes, interests, and ideas of others whenever possible. In this scenario, you are clearly demonstrating that you are going for a win-win.

The relationship message you are sending is that you see yourself as a constructive leader and/or an 'active' person, and that you see the other person as someone who needs guidance and/or help. This will trigger others to show respect and follow you with green behaviour.

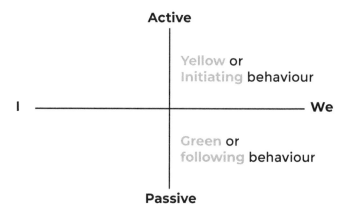

Figure 10.3 Constructive following behaviour (green)

The next type of behaviour is the combination of passive and "we" behaviour. This is called green, or following behaviour (green is a symbol for positive collaboration; for wanting to follow and to learn from others). The behaviour you are showing demonstrates that you are doing this because you want to. And often you want to because you feel invited to do so. The relationship message you are sending here is, "I am a friendly and constructive person, willing to accept help, advice, and instructions." The behaviour you will trigger towards yourself is yellow behaviour, namely people giving you advice, instructions, guidance, and help.

This also means that, if you have the feeling that everybody is always helping, guiding, or instructing you, then it is possible that you are provoking this. Indeed, passive behaviour evokes active behaviour.

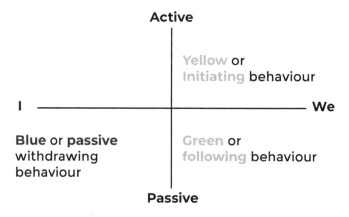

Figure 10.4 Passive withdrawing behaviour (blue)

Next is the passive "I" corner, which is called blue behaviour, or passive withdrawing behaviour (blue because it is often a bit more cold and distant). Mainly, you keep quiet and/or you make some, but not a lot, of critical remarks. You show your disagreement non-verbally, and do not verbalise the fact that you have different ideas. You sigh, frown, doodle, and laugh in a slightly cynical way. The relationship message you are sending with this behaviour is, "I don't feel secure, I have rather low self-esteem at this moment, I don't trust you, and I am a bit cynical about your good intentions." This triggers red behaviour: pushing, ignoring, or arguing.

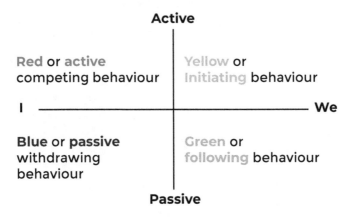

Active

Red or active
competing behaviour

Yellow or
Initiating behaviour

I ——————————————— We

Blue or passive
withdrawing
behaviour

Green or
following behaviour

Passive

Figure 10.5 Active competing behaviour (red)

Now we arrive at the upper left corner, which we call red behaviour, or competitive behaviour. The red stands for the passion and fire that often goes along with this position. Here you are active, and directly defend your own position. The behaviour you show includes arguing, talking a lot, not listening, and not giving people a lot of space to discuss their ideas. The relationship message you are sending is, "I know better, I am right, and I have the best idea or solution." The behaviour this attitude triggers is often blue behaviour, which first includes some rebellion, and then people retreat and become passive and cynical.

The Leadership Compass and the "Iron lady"

I had been working for a global food company for several years. The consulting consisted of leadership development on several levels. At a certain point we did a 'train the trainer' programme for senior management.

A magical thing happened in one of the 'train the trainer' sessions. Present was a woman named Michelle who had a reputation. I had never met her personally but, as we had been working with this company for several years, we heard a lot of stories about her. She was disrespectfully labelled as "The Iron Lady, ruling the African continent." When Michelle entered the training room, we could see immediately that there was a lot going on inside of her; she seemed to be in a state of personal development. During the training we used a version of the Leadership Compass, and this seemed to be a very important trigger for her to further question herself. The Leadership Compass shows how your behaviour influences others, and vice versa.

With our feedback, she realised that, as she evolved in her career, she'd developed a 'red' behaviour, which means that she was primarily very active and dominant, defending and pushing her own perspective on others. She did not hesitate to tackle people in an aggressive way. What shocked me was how this behaviour was stimulated and reinforced by her male colleagues. They would often make remarks like, "Come on Michelle, go and get them." After the training, she was coached by a colleague of mine and she had a real breakthrough. She even visited different teams to apologize for her past behaviour. She became a great leader and a great advocate for the 'train the trainers' programme.

Being too active as a leader will make others too passive.

Based on Timothy Leary

CHAPTER ELEVEN

Core Intervention Skills: Using the Leadership Compass in Daily Practice

In this chapter, I show how to apply, in real life and in a practical way, the Leadership Compass tool described in Chapter Ten. I describe the different skills you can use to shape action and reaction. These interventions are a clear and specific behaviour you can show, in order to steer an interaction in the desired way. I will frequently refer to the case: Guiding Hossein to overcome a major threshold in coaching others. For each skill I describe, I refer to videos (Demo Video: Guiding Hossein) on my website, www.mindgrowing.net, that exemplify the techniques I use.

I follow a pathway that is very useful when you feel that people are in a more defensive mode towards a certain change, project, decision, or solution (these are in the blue area). You can influence people to move in any horizontal or vertical direction within the Leadership Compass, but you can only make one move at a time. So, if you say or do something, which I have labelled as a skill or 'intervention', you can, for example, move a person or (part of) a team from:

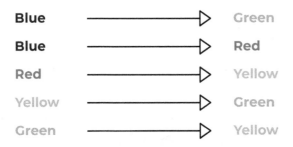

Blue	⟶	Green
Blue	⟶	Red
Red	⟶	Yellow
Yellow	⟶	Green
Green	⟶	Yellow

Guiding Hossein to overcome a major threshold in coaching others

The following case is based on one of my coachings. In the demo video on the website I play the role of Hossein's manager. Hossein is an engineer at a chemical production plant. He has extremely good technical knowledge and has a strong ability to solve technical problems. In this sense, Hossein is an employee who adds great value. At one point, a younger woman named Sophia started as a trainee. To develop Hossein's social skills, he was asked to train and coach her, so that she could get up to speed as soon as possible. However, Hossein is not doing it. When speaking to Sophia, she says that Hossein does not talk to her or give her any information. He answers her technical questions, but he does not give her any tasks or instructions to develop her abilities and skills. When speaking to Hossein about this he becomes rather negative and even a bit cynical.

I will try to understand what is happening, and see how Hossein can be helped to coach Sophia, using the Leadership Compass tool.

However, in my experience, within a change process—both individual and organisational—people often start in the blue area because they are a bit defensive and sceptical thinking, "Oh, not another change," "Not again," or "We never finish something." Only a few people clearly and explicitly express these thoughts, which would put them in the red area. And, of course, there are always people in the green and yellow area, taking initiative and building the road ahead. But, when there is a person or group in the blue area, I have discovered that it is often more effective to first get them to the red area, thereby making them active and expressing their concerns and feedback. Then, by taking their concerns and ideas seriously, you can pull them towards the "we" side. However, once there, sometimes these people become too active and start formulating all kinds of solutions which are not realistic or feasible at that moment. Then your challenge is to make them a little less active without pushing them back to the "I" side i.e. the red and blue corners. This is the exact path I want to follow when talking with Hossein.

The Core Intervention Skills

Below you will find a series of different scenarios that help to illustrate each of the skills I use to move people from one corner of the Leadership Compass to another.

Moving Someone from Blue to Red Behaviour
This involves moving someone from blue (passive resistant) to red (active resistant) behaviour, to make someone silent speak their mind.

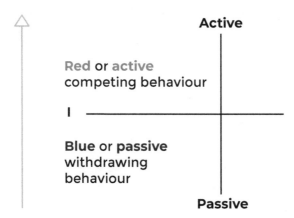

Figure 11.1 From blue to red behaviour

Indicate behaviour
You sigh, what happens?

Indicating a behaviour is when you describe a certain behaviour to an employee and ask why it is happening—and then be silent. Indicating behaviour is a very strong technique that makes people reflect and also react. It is important that you make your statement and then stay silent. If you continue talking, you remain active, which makes the other person passive instead of active.

In the video clip online I ask, "Hossein you're sighing, what's going on?"

Questions and more questions
Why? How? What?

This is all about **questioning and active listening.**

Do you remember the New Leadership ABCs? You have to offer three key elements to people in order to lead them in the best way: purpose or ambition, boundaries, and coaching.

What I often try to do with my questioning is to find out which of these three things are not working for someone. I try to find out if the person still shares my purpose and ambition. I also try to find out if there is a problem with boundaries, theirs or mine.

In the video online, I ask Hossein a lot of questions about why he doesn't seem to be happy coaching Sophia, or with my leadership. Does he have the time, the means, and the skills? Does coaching her align with his values? For example, if he really believes that he does not have the professional skills to coach someone, then he can tell me that I am violating his boundaries.

Lower the treshold
Please speak, perhaps I am wrong

To make people more active in the conversation, you can lower the threshold to speak, by stressing the importance for you of knowing what they think and feel, or by showing your own vulnerability. In the video, I stress the fact that it is important to me that Hossein expresses himself, that he is happy in his work, and that I would like to help him if I can.

Moving Someone from Red to Yellow Behaviour

This involves moving someone from red ("I"/active) to yellow ("we"/active) behaviour, to pull someone focused on competition towards collaboration.

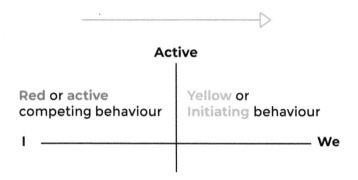

Figure 11.2 Moving from red to yellow behaviour

 Acknowledge
Thanks for sharing, I see that, I agree

Acknowledge wherever possible. Do this only when you mean it, but do it! We often say what we don't agree about; here you should say explicitly what you do agree about. This will show other persons that you understand them, and that you can and want to see their perspective. This will pull the other person strongly to the "we" side. In the video, I tell Hossein that I agree with him that he has a lot of work in the technical field.

Questions
More questions about what their concerns are exactly, what works for them and what doesn't.

Ask a lot of questions. This remains a great skill to be used. Try to discover as much as you can, specifically if the problem is situated on the goal level ("I don't share the ambition/purpose"), at the boundaries level ("I don't have the means or skills," or, "It is against my values, beliefs, and emotions"), or at the coaching level ("I need help to find a way to do it.")

Check Purpose
Do we still share the same purpose

I have already mentioned this skill, but it deserves special attention. It is **checking on your common purpose**. It means that you check, in an explicit way, if you and your interaction partner are still after the same goal or ambition. If this is not the case, and if you share the ambition but you disagree on how best to achieve it (which is more on the level of boundaries and coaching), then you need to have a totally different conversation.

Acknowledge the intent
Okay, you want to do it in a professional way.

Asking questions and active listening remain some of the core skills you can use. A strong skill to add, however, is to **summarise the intent and core interests** of the other person. For example, "So, if I understand you correctly, what you are saying is that it is important for you that the introduction of new people should be professionalized. Okay, I share that feeling." From here you can make an easy transition to a win-win result by saying, "We both share the same intent, now let's see how we can find a way to get there that suits us both."

Calming Over-active Yellow Behaviour
This involves moving someone demonstrating yellow behaviour from being too active on the "we" side i.e. too many non-feasible ideas, to being more focused on a win-win i.e. deactivating them a little bit.

Figure 11.3 Deactivating yellow behaviour towards more collaboration

As I described above, whenever possible, try to summarize the real intent of the other person and acknowledge it. You might say, "Okay, so you want to do it in a more professional way? I encourage that, and I agree. I share that interest with you."

Frame
There are also boundaries: time, money, core values...

It is also important to **frame the boundaries**. You, as a leader, also have boundaries which need to be respected. In the video I say, "On the other hand, I have a budget and a time limit and, next to professionalism, finding quick and practical solutions is also a core value of mine and of our company. So, can we discuss how to realise you coaching Sophia, within the boundaries you and I find important?"

Create a win-win
Okay, how can we keep your intent/interest and find a way to realise it within the boundaries?

In order to **discover a win-win approach**, seriously explore how you can find a solution that respects Hossein's core intent, and fits within his boundaries and yours.

But now, let's go back in time and suppose that, at the beginning of our conversation, Hossein is not in the blue corner but in the green corner. He shows constructive following behaviour; he acknowledges that he has to coach Sophia, and you have the impression that he really wants to. On the other hand, you doubt that he will take any initiative once he has left the room. So, now I will try to activate him so that he will show some more initiative.

"Activating" Passive Green Behaviour
Moving someone on the "we" side from passive to more active; encouraging someone with green behaviour, who is likely to follow, to take more initiative.

Figure 11.4 Encouraging someone with green behaviour to be more 'active'

Questions to gauge concerns
Why? How? What?

As I indicated earlier, you can **ask questions** about a lot of different things. Here, I mainly ask questions to find out if there are concerns or other blocking factors that are preventing Hossein from taking initiative. Once I know these, we can try to find solutions for them, and thus remove them.

Acknowledge
Indeed, it was very busy, I see that

It is always important to **acknowledge** the things you recognize and/or share. It is a strong skill to stay on the "we" side.

Frame
State boundaries: 'Sit with Sophia this week'

Framing is also used to give a little pressure and a sense of urgency. In the role play I say to Hossein: "I want to plan a short meeting with you every week". When a person is showing behaviour in the green corner, it is important not to do too much framing, as it will make you active or dominant and your employee passive, which is the opposite of what you want. Just a bit of framing is needed, to create a bit more urgency. When someone is really not showing any sign of taking initiative, then it can be very effective to state a boundary that contains at least minimal action to get the person going. In this case, by saying to Hossein that I expect him to sit down with Sophia this week, I am attempting to boost his initiative.

Reflective questions
'How do you want to organize the first talk?'

In order to develop following behaviour into a more permanent modus of taking initiative, it is very important to **guide someone through reflective questions** when learning, which at the same time will help them find solutions themselves. If you, as a leader, dictate all solutions, then the other person will stay as passive as you are active. However, you can make people think by asking questions like "How would you approach this task?" "What do you see as the main hurdles here?" and "How do you want to take this on?"

However, sometimes you can overdo it with reflective questions. It is often good to give the other person some **tools or more specific instructions** to find a solution. If you don't, the situation can become too open and frustrating for your employee. One warning: if you give specific instructions, make sure to stop giving instructions after one or two instances. To make this clear, you can say something like, "As you are inexperienced in this new task, I will give you instructions to help you find solutions. However, within a few weeks I will stop giving specific instructions, and I expect you to develop the initiative to find your own way." This can be a real downside of instructions. A lot of people like to follow them because then they don't have to take responsibility themselves. If they do this, then they don't develop, and they will stay dependent on your instructions.

The Emergency Brake
Finally, let's look at an approach that I call your emergency brake. What if the person you are managing is not willing to move, and is stuck in passive or active resistant behaviour, or is too dominant or too passive and not receptive to the skills we discussed?

In the video, I say the following to Hossein, "I am sorry Hossein; We are talking for a while but we are not moving. So, if you don't want me to help you, we have to stop. So, for you the choice is either you let me help you and you work with me, or we stop here. But, please take into account that stopping will not mean that my expectations towards you will change, as my ambition is not negotiable. However, we can talk about how to achieve this, and I am willing to help if you want."

If you feel that this is too long, then start with, "Hossein, if you continue like this then it stops." Then, silence! I am 99 per cent sure that he will ask, "What do you mean?" Then you can explain, as described above.

The main skill I use here is what I call meta-communication. I take some psychological distance, and from a meta-level I describe how I see the communication progressing. Along with this, I describe the consequences this will have for me and for him. Here you can be very strict and tough. As a leader, your ambitions and core boundaries and values are not negotiable!

In summary, leading is all about finding the right balance between leading and following behaviour, in order to develop skilled, engaged, autonomous people who connect to your ambition and are willing to work within the defined playing field.

The guiding principles are:

• First follow, then lead.

• First understand, then be understood.

It is a dance where leading and following are intertwined towards creating a great dialogue.

The following chart describes the different approaches you can take. In the left column you find the main behaviours which can be considered as leading. You use them to steer the interaction in the right direction. In the right column you see the following behaviours. As a leader you use them to truly engage people by giving space, showing respect, and taking into account their interests, ideas and concerns.

LEADING	FOLLOWING
Indicate behaviour; mention the facts, numbers, and examples you observe.	Ask questions. And then ask more questions to explore the interests and boundaries of the other person.
Lower the threshold for discussion; encourage and show your own vulnerability to create a safe space to speak.	Acknowledge when someone is right.
Check ambition, and regularly check if the ambition is still shared; if not, everything else will make little sense.	Ask more questions.
Frame and formulate your boundaries—the playing field that needs to be respected.	Acknowledge the intent of the other person, their core interests, and look beyond what they are proposing as a solution, to what they really want.
Create a win-win approach; tell and show that you want to find an integration of interests.	Ask questions to find concerns.
Ask reflective questions to make the other person think.	
Give clear and detailed instructions when necessary.	

Figure 11.5 A summary of leading and following intervention skills

Exercise: Reflect on the Core Skills to Influence Dynamics Within a Talk or Meeting

Think about the conversations you have with people you manage and rate to what extent you use the different skills described below.

SKILLS	OFTEN	SOMETIMES	SELDOM
Indicating behaviour: You give descriptive factual feedback about the behaviour you see. For example, "You frown, what is happening?"			
Asking questions to understand the viewpoint of the other person, and what they are thinking and feeling. For example, "How do you see it?"			
Lowering the threshold, and actively encouraging people to speak their minds. For example, "Please tell me what you think, it is important to me."			
Stopping to check in, to see if people are still sharing the same ambition as you. For example, "Do you still agree with our goal?"			
Acknowledging that the other person has a good point, or that they are right. For example, "Yes, you are right."			

SKILLS	OFTEN	SOMETIMES	SELDOM
Acknowledging the intent, values and core interests of others. For example, "I hear that you find quality important; me too."			
Framing or stating your playing field as a leader. For example, "We must stay within budget and we need to align with other departments."			
Asking questions to hear concerns. For example, "What is on your mind? Please tell me your concerns."			
Explicitly stating that you want a win-win situation. For example, "With the ambition in mind, and within the playing field, I really want to find a way to serve all of our interests."			
Asking reflective questions. For example, "How do you want to approach this task?"			
Giving specific and detailed instructions. For example, "When doing this task, please follow the manual, step by step."			

Which skills do you want to develop? Describe how and when.

Skills I want to develop	Why do I want to develop this skill?	Choose a specific situation and person for which you think applying this skill could make a difference? For example, "In my weekly talk with Robert..."	When and where are you going to apply it?

The Leadership Compass Concept Applied to a Team

I've explained the action/reaction dynamic, demonstrated in the concept of the Leadership Compass, and its application in a face-to-face interaction. However, these same dynamics are also applicable to team interaction, and even on an organisational level between, for example, different departments. Let's look at how it can be applied to a team.

Whenever a team is interacting, like during a meeting, different people will be in different corners of the Compass at different moments. As an example, you might be discussing the strategy for the coming year. I can suppose that some or most of your team members are offering ideas and input (they are in the yellow corner). Others are listening and nodding, so it is likely that they are in the green, or following, corner. However, this is sometimes difficult to be sure of. When people are quiet, it is hard to know if they are at the "I" side (they still have their own ideas, but are not expressing themselves) or the "we" side (they are thinking and working along with the group). So, it is always good to make them active and to check, with the following question, "May I ask you to share your thoughts with us?" Perhaps some of your team members are in the blue corner. They are not saying a lot, but non-verbally you can see that they are not happy, are not agreeing with what is being said, or with how the meeting is going. And, of course, I can imagine that there are also people who, while showing red behaviour, are opposing the ideas of others, and defending their own ideas and vision with arguments. This is fine, as long as people don't get stuck in a corner, blocking the team dynamics and the decision-making or creative process.

A team needs opposition and competition to create fire, creativity, and innovation. Let me stress again that someone might have a clear presence in one of the corners, but, in general, people move around these four corners during a meeting. The yellow, the green, the blue, and the red are behaviours and not people. But most people will have a tendency to be more in one corner than other corners. As long as people are moving around in the different corners, showing different kinds of behaviours, your meeting is probably going well. You will have a good mix of ideas, opposing behaviours, followers and executers, and people looking a bit annoyed at certain points. However, when more people seem to be stuck in a certain corner, then it could become a problem. If the same patterns occur, in the same way, in different meetings, then this could mean that your team is stuck in a fixed interaction pattern. When this is an effective pattern, delivering good results and happy team members, then, of course, there is no problem. But this is not always easy to discern.

After a while, most teams, if not every team, creates a kind of fixed pattern. Some people are always the active ones, most of the others are followers, with some of them often in the active or passive opposition. And, if you look at the concept, this is logical. Active people will fill the space, either in an "I" or a "we" way, making others more passive. The same is true the other way around: passive people in the group will always trigger the active ones to take initiative very quickly. The problem with this is that possibilities often get lost when nothing changes. If the same people are always active, passive, opposing, or collaborating, then you will probably always have the same pattern and the same output. It would be very interesting to see what would happen if you could make passive people a bit more active, and vice versa, and make similar changes to the "I-we" dynamic.

Leading and managing these kinds of interactions within your team is one of the core responsibilities of a leader. But, everyone within the team has a responsibility; to be aware of, and to contribute to, healthy, balanced, and effective interaction patterns. There are different things that you, as leader, can do to change and create interaction within your team. You can also use a lot of the skills I discussed in Chapter Nine in a team setting. But, in this case, you should use the following actions and initiatives that use the principles of the New Leadership ABCs.

Team Coaching: Combining the New Leadership ABCs and the Leadership Compass

Figure 11.6 Three core elements to build a high performing team

Ambition

The basis for a high performing team is a strong ambition, in the sense of a common purpose, which is clear and shared by everyone (see Chapter Six), and translated into team and individual goals.

Boundaries

Make sure that the boundaries are clear. In order to reach the ambition, it is important to make sure that tasks and roles within the team are clear and transparent. When a team is new, or major changes have been made to its composition, it is wise that you, as a leader, take the lead to lay down these goals and the division of tasks. It will give the team members the structure that is necessary to feel safe, and to develop their own ideas, thoughts, and initiatives. If these things are not clear, the team members tend to stay occupied with these fundamental but elementary aspects. In contrast, when they are clear, the team will have energy to develop a dynamic which will be more focused on how to get results. At a certain point, they will probably also start to challenge the ambition and the boundaries you defined, and that's fine. It is a sign that dynamics are evolving in the right direction. Wherever possible, listen to team members and take into account whatever they suggest, if it is acceptable and fits within your ambition and boundaries. If not, explain in a very clear way why it is not possible.

Culture and Coaching

It is a logical, and even necessary, step for people to disagree and have conflict. There will be very different views on how to handle rules: Should you be strict or flexible? How standardised do they have to be? On which level of detail do you need to discuss them? When you see that these differences arise, don't push them away. Put them, in a calm and very objective way, on the table. Describe what you see and invite people to talk about it. For example, I may hear from Marc that he wants to follow rules strictly, and I may hear from Fatima that she wants some flexibility in applying some rules. How should I deal with this? You could have a fundamental discussion about how the rules will be applied in this team. Once you have had a good and fulfilling discussion, with a clear conclusion, this should not come up again, unless perhaps there are some major changes to the composition of your team. If, after a while, you find that these discussions and conflicts on different subjects keep appearing, it would be wise to look for some guidance from your HR department. It is the role of a leader to handle differences, opinions, and even conflicts. However, when they escalate it is time to ask for guidance. One good indicator of when to ask for guidance, is when discussions move from discussing content to making personal remarks or attacks.

The main challenge is not to choose one or the other (unless it is really necessary), but instead to find a way of handling conflicts in such a way that they lead to integration and synthesis, gaining profit from differences. It is this feeling, that it is possible to handle differences in a mature, open, and adult way leading to synthesis, that will make a high-performing team. Handling differences of opinion and conflicts are some of the core skills to develop as a leader.

There are also some practical things you can do to lead and influence the dynamics within your team:

- **Indicate patterns you see:** this is what I just described when talking about putting a conflict on the table. You can also use this when you see a pattern that you think is probably not effective. For example, when the same two people are always super active (yellow corner), you might say, "I notice, during this meeting, that Ahmed is offering a lot of ideas, and that the others are keeping quiet. What's happening?"

- You can also **give feedback**, "Ahmed, I see that you are very involved and active, but may I ask you to wait for a moment, so that others can first give their ideas?"

- When you have a team of very passive and quiet people (in the green and blue corner), you can use some techniques to **lower the threshold**. For example, when discussing a very important topic, first let people discuss in small groups, and have them write their ideas, questions, or remarks on a post-it note. Collect the post-it notes and categorise them on a flipchart. Then, discuss the different topics, and see if you get a more balanced and animated exchange.

- When one or two persons move to the "I"/active corner (red behaviour, opposing and/or defending their own ideas), there are different possibilities for intervention:

  - Take some time to explore their arguments, and use the skills described in this chapter: ask questions, explore their interest and boundaries, and check to see if they still share the ambition. Often, they have a good reason to oppose or discuss. If you find this reason, and you will, integrate it and come to a better solution, approach, or plan. The challenge here is to take some time to do the right thing for the people opposing and arguing, without spending too much time on it and annoying the others. In a case where there are only one or two, and you have the strong feeling that the others are with you, then don't take more than five minutes to explore the view of those in opposition before continuing with your meeting.

- Sometimes you should wait a bit, and see if the others react. Often when you, as a leader, start having a discussion with a small group of people, it can become annoying for the others, certainly when it takes too much time. However, very often you see that the team corrects its own members, but you have to give them the opportunity. You can also consider asking explicitly what the others think about the vision or position that has been formulated.

- If someone goes overboard, correct them and ask them to stop. Speak with them afterwards, individually.

It is very important, when creating the desired culture within your team, to make sure that the basic boundaries you have defined are embedded. For example, these might be as follows.

It is not acceptable:

- not to ask for help when needed.

- not to share knowledge and experience.

- that results are attained at the expense of others.

It is crucial that, whenever your team is interacting, you are very attentive to the fact that these boundaries are respected. Each time— and to be honest, one time is enough—that they are not applied, and you don't react, you are demolishing your desired culture. This is really fundamental. You either give the message that they are core principles, or your message is the opposite, "Yes, there are some boundaries, but that's only to keep up appearances."

Exercise: **Have a Look at Your Own Team**

A fun and effective way to develop your team is to visualise how the team dynamics are at this moment.

Get a white sheet of paper. Write down the names of all team members, including yourself. See below for an example. Put them at a certain distance from each other: the closer they are on paper, the closer they are in reality. Represent them either as a circle (when they are easy to lead and coach), or with sharp edges (when they are difficult). The size of the shape should represent their impact within the team. The bigger the impact, the bigger the shape. Connect people with a straight line if they have a good relationship. Use a jagged line when the relationship is troubled, or full of conflict. Use a dotted line when you think that they need to work together more.

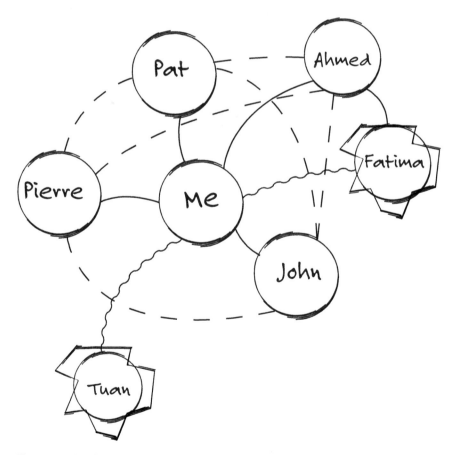

Figure 11.7 Visualising team dynamics

Here are some examples of what this visualisation above could tell us:

1. The leader (me) is in the middle of a group of people. There is a good relationship between me and the other people on the team, but it seems that they are hardly working together (see the dotted lines). So, I can see that I need to stimulate collaboration between these people.

2. At this moment, it looks like everything is passing through me, the leader. This will limit the possibilities of the team.

3. Probably the biggest insight here, is that I need to have a good look at how I am leading this team. It is also important that I involve Ahmed in this group, but not Fatima. I have a troubled relationship with her, and she has a big impact, and is difficult to coach. She is close to Ahmed, so the questions are: What is happening with Fatima? What is her influence on Ahmed, and vice versa? How can this help or block Ahmed's integration into the group? Is it still the aim to integrate Fatima, or is that not desirable anymore?

4. And then, of course, there is Juan? What is happening there?

Now, take some time to make the same analysis for your team. Don't think too much. Just follow your intuition and make the visualisation. When it is finished, try to draw conclusions, and look at the tools above for possible interventions you could use with your team. When this is finished, I highly recommend asking a HR business partner, or another senior person with extensive experience leading teams, to consult on your analysis and to discuss the actions you might want to take. Also, reflect on your work in other exercises in this book as all of them are connected!

Ask yourself the following questions:

- How is your ambition reflected in this picture, and are the team dynamics helping to realise it?

- Are boundaries clear, supported and respected?

- What is the culture you want to build?

- What do different people need to develop (i.e. awareness, willingness, ability, courage)?

- How are your leadership skills (refer to the Leadership Compass), and how do they interplay with this picture?

In the next chapter, I will describe two core tools that summarize a lot of the skills mentioned in this book, which you can use to structure your effort. They can offer you a strong framework when developing your people, team and culture.

Summarizing the Core of the New Leadership ABCs: Creating Emotional Gravity and Steering with Company DNA

So, what is the relevance of the New Leadership ABCs? As stated earlier, ambition must come from the heart and, even more important, it has to be genuine. If your ambition doesn't come from the heart and isn't genuine, it will never have the power to attach people to it emotionally. In the New Leadership ABCs, ambition, together with coaching and culture, must have the power of emotional gravity that connects, attracts, and keeps people in the right orbit to realise the ambition of your company. The boundaries can be seen as the fundamental laws that define how far people can deviate in their behaviour and actions when realising the ambition. Boundaries must be a kind of DNA that is present in each and every action of all employees. Each action will carry the stamp of the boundaries.

So, emotional gravity is nothing more or less than the emotional and loyal connection of people to a genuine ambition that gives purpose and meaning. The company DNA is the code that guides this freed energy in the right direction.

No shine without friction.

CHAPTER TWELVE

The New Leadership ABCs Summarized in Two Tools

Until now, I have been describing the New Leadership ABCs as a core concept to shape your leadership. But, over the years, I have translated this concept into two core tools. These tools can be used for many different situations where you want to create buy-in, engagement, and ownership, to solve problems or to attain goals. They can be used in face-to-face talks, in meetings, or even in large group settings. They also work well for solving current operational problems, and for structuring longer-term change processes.

The two tools are meant for two fundamentally different situations:

The first, called the **New Leadership ABCs: From Challenge to Solution**, can be used whenever you have the opportunity to share a challenge or problem with people, and allows them to contribute to shaping the way forward and finding solutions. These tools respect the elements of SCARF to the fullest. Sharing a challenge or problem, and taking people seriously in their ability to find solutions within certain boundaries, will boost their status, autonomy, and relatedness. Therefore, I advise you to use it as much as possible.

However, sometimes a solution or future plan is already decided, and the only option is to implement it. In a situation like this, there is less space for people to have autonomy in creating their own way forward. In that sense, SCARF will be less respected, as people become executers of a solution decided for them and not with them.

The second tool is called the **New Leadership ABCs: From Decision to Acceptance**. It gives people, in a controlled way, the opportunity to contribute when a decision is fixed, and a solution is being implemented. It respects the elements of SCARF, as much as possible, given that the decision itself is already made and will not change.

Tool One: The New Leadership ABCs: From Challenge to Solution

When using this tool, you should structure a meeting (or several meetings) according to the New Leadership ABCs. You should first talk about the ambition, then create a playing field by stating and explaining the boundaries, and finally you should offer the floor to employees to find solutions. An essential principle is to make sure that, with every step, you have buy-in.

Take this theoretical example of a problem to be solved. As a leader, you notice that, during the last six months, the percentage of complaints from customers is slowly increasing by two per cent every month.

First, focus on the A.

A: Present the Challenge/Problem in Light of the Ambition

Link your problem or challenge (that complaints are increasing each month by two per cent) to the ambition of the team, and then do a stop-and-check. Imagine that the ambition of the team is "to provide products and services that make people smile." In this case, you can prepare a meeting with your team and the introduction could be framed as follows:

> "We are all working to realise our ambition to provide products and services that make people smile. I had a look at the numbers, and I noticed that the complaints are rising by two per cent each month. I think we have to solve this. Do you agree? What do you think?"

To make sure that your message will have the right impact, it is good to translate your message into two or three shocking facts. Don't be vague by saying, "We get too many complaints," or, "We have to work on our customer service to lower the number of complaints." Instead, use some shocking, awareness-creating numbers that awaken the crocodile brain. For example:

- "Every month, we add 50 people to the group of non-smiling customers."

- "The amount of non-smiling customers who don't return to us is 80 per cent."

- "It costs us, on average, $3,500 to acquire a new customer."

The responses you receive from your team can vary, but here are some of the most likely things you will hear:

1. They will say yes, this is a problem, that it must be solved, and they will look for solutions.

2. They say yes, this is a problem, but it has nothing to do with us, and/or we are not the ones who can solve it.

3. They will say no, this is not a problem, because there are many good reasons to explain this rise in complaints.

If you get the first response, perfect! Go to B, the boundaries, and then look for solutions and offer coaching where necessary

If you get the second or third response, that's less than perfect, but not to worry. Say that your intention is just to check if people agree with the fact that this is happening (the increase in complaints), and that it is not OK for the team or the company, regardless of the cause. The cause is not as important at this moment; being on the same page about this being undesirable is.

When speaking at the ambition-level, it is not useful to start analysing the problem, or discussing the causes for the problem. On the contrary, this can often be counterproductive and could shift the focus away from sharing a sense of urgency.

Later, when you start looking for solutions, is the best time to analyse and discuss the causes of the problem.

The next thing to do, at the ambition-level, is to present and mutually agree on a clear goal. In this example, this could be, "Let's make sure that, within two months, the monthly increase in complaints is stopped—so a zero per cent increase—and, after that, there will be a further decrease of one per cent a month. Our aim is to have more smiling customers."

B: Present and Check Boundaries

Now, present your boundaries. State within which playing field people can find solutions. You need to prepare this before the meeting.

You might say something like, "I expect you to find solutions for this problem, but with the following conditions:

1. We have to move quickly. The first solutions must be implemented within two weeks.

2. We have a budget of $50. We can use it, but we can't spend more than that.

3. We can't come up with solutions that create problems for other departments."

Present your boundaries, and then check with your team. Ask them if they can see that these boundaries are important. Ask them if they clearly define the playing field, and whether they see that they offer a lot of possibilities, but also some restrictions. Check to make sure they understand the restrictions.

What often happens at this point, is that employees start to formulate their own boundaries. For example, they might say, "We could work on that if we can spend a few hours per week on it," or, "This means that we have to reconsider our current priorities." Make sure that you understand exactly what they mean, why they're saying it, and whether it is something you can accommodate. If possible, do accommodate or take it into account. The worst thing you can do is to present yourself as having a big ego, defending everything you propose. Pick your battles and defend your core ambition and boundaries. It is very positive if, at this point, you are able to have a strong but mature discussion about which boundaries are feasible and whether they can be negotiated. If this takes place, the acceptance of the ambition and boundaries will only be greater, and the solutions will come. What you are doing is taking your position as a leader seriously (you say what you want, and within which boundaries), but you are also respecting the principles of SCARF by allowing this mature discussion with your employees.

C: Formulate and Check What Coaching People Require to Find Solutions

The direction is set and the framing is done. Now it is time to see where your team and its members need coaching and support. Perhaps they don't! In that case, let them go ahead and create, but make some agreements on how a follow-up will be organised (when, how, how often, and with whom).

When you're working on a specific project or a certain task, it is wise to regularly estimate, in general, if all team members are ready for the work ahead. You should ask if your team is:

1. **Aware:** Do they see the importance of the ambition and the boundaries?

2. **Willing:** Are they truly willing and motivated to find solutions?

3. **Skilled:** Do they have the knowledge and skills needed to find and/or implement solutions?

4. **Daring:** Are there any moments that ask for courage, and do they have it? If not, can you support them?

These four aspects, discussed in more detail in Chapter Eight, are an easy to remember tool to make sure that people are ready to attain the goals you've defined. It is much more likely that the goal will be achieved if these four elements are present within individuals and teams.

If these elements aren't present, then it is your task to make sure that support will be offered. It isn't really necessary for a leader to do the coaching and development themselves. You just have to make sure that it happens, and provide the necessary means. You can ask employees to help each other within the team, or across departments. You could also use formal existing training, online training, in-person training, or ask HR for assistance.

Here is a summary of tool one:

From Challenge to Solution:

Creating ownership
Whenever there is a problem to solve and an ambition to realise, and you have the opportunity to let people come up with the way to do it, then use this process. I understand that this is not always possible because a solution might have already been decided somewhere within the organisation.

First, explain the aim and the structure of the meeting, then follow the next steps:

Step one: Ambition

Present the challenge/problem in terms of shocking facts, linked to your ambition.
Check to make sure they understand that these facts are a problem.
Present a goal to reach.
Check to make sure everyone sees the importance of the goal.

Step two: Boundaries

Present the playing field i.e. the boundaries (including possibilities and limitations).
Check to make sure everyone sees the importance of these boundaries.

Step three: Coaching

Let them find solutions and actions.
Offer coaching and other support when needed.
Organise follow-ups and monitor.

Tool Two: **The New Leadership ABCs: From Decision to Acceptance**

Tool two is meant for situations where a top-down approach is needed. Sometimes this is more appropriate for certain changes, like the introduction of new software, new systems, or for a structural reorganisation. However, it is good to realise that a top-down approach, however necessary, is less likely to respect the SCARF elements. So, make sure that you create time and opportunities to add them to the equation, by having a dialogue.

The biggest difference from tool one will be that this dialogue is not about how to shape the change fundamentally (like in a bottom-up approach), but is instead about how a change is going to be implemented. For example, what are the concerns and difficulties people see and feel, and what can be done to minimise them or take them away? So, here the dialogue is more about finding the best and most comfortable way of implementing the change. If you do this with integrity, and not just as a trick (for example, giving people the opportunity to vent, and then forgetting about it), it will make all the difference, even if you can only solve some of the concerns, and not all. If people feel that you, as a leader, really try, and they feel it with their limbic brain, then they will at least trust you, which is one of the core elements in the willingness to follow a leader. The opposite, of course, is that you follow a leader out of fear.

Again, we will start with the ambition-level.

A: Present the Challenge/Problem in Light of the Ambition
This part is similar to tool one. Describe the ambition of your team or organisation, and link shocking facts and solutions in one short communication, to kick-start the talk or meeting.

For example, you might say, "As you know, it is our mission to make our customers smile. However, right now we are seeing the number of complaints increasing by two per cent each month. The goal is to stop this increase within two months. From there, we would like to realise a decrease in complaints by one per cent per month."

Now, do a stop-and-check, "Do you also feel or agree that this is a serious challenge we have to tackle?"

As with tool one, people can respond in different ways to this.

B: Present and Check Boundaries

Now, present the boundaries, and, in this case, they are rather high, mainly because the solution has already been decided. Briefly explain the solution and its consequences. Don't defend the solution with arguments or its advantages. You will be talking to the rational brain and ignoring the limbic brain. Say that this solution is decided and fixed. However, also stress that you can imagine it's likely there are some concerns. State that, if there are ways to tackle these concerns and to minimise them within existing boundaries (time, budget, core values, etc.), everything will be done to resolve them. Also, state within which boundaries support can be offered. For example, you might say, "We have an implementation budget of $50," or "We cannot cause problems in other departments."

Now ask them to put all their concerns on the table. List them, ask questions, and be sure that you capture the core of their concerns. Write them on a flip chart, or on a white board. Don't stop until all concerns are listed. Then go to C.

Here is an example of what you might say, "We analysed the situation, and the management team has decided that it is wise to organise training for customer-focused behaviour. So, in the coming month, each of you will go through this training. I can imagine that you have concerns and feelings about this. Please share them with me. I will try to understand them, I'll write them all down, and then afterwards we will see if we can do something about them, within the possibilities available to us. But first, please let me know what you are feeling and thinking." At this point, there should be no discussion and no arguments; only listen and ask questions to better understand their concerns and feelings.

C: Explore Coaching and the Support People Require to Implement the Solution in an Engaged Way

Now, have a look at their concerns. Categorise them and brainstorm with the team on how you can best deal with them. Ask people if they have ideas about what could solve their concerns. Again, not all concerns can be, or have to be, resolved. Just help and support your people wherever you can. That will be enough! Also, you don't have to do all the work. If members of the team have their own ideas, and can shape the solutions themselves, let them do it. Just make sure that the boundaries are well defined.

For example, some of the concerns voiced may include:
1. "We already did some restructuring, and it didn't help."

2. "Restructuring takes time and energy that we could be spending on customers."

3. "I don't want to move to another branch because I have young children and it is stressful to change schools. Also, my partner has a good job that we cannot afford to lose."

4. "It takes so much energy to change roles and positions."

When the list is complete, it is time to brainstorm and have a dialogue, within the boundaries, about solutions to some of the concerns. You might ask some of the following questions:

1. "Is there anything we can do to make this restructuring more successful than the ones in the past?" (Note that here a dialogue might begin about lessons learned from the past, and how to use them for the future).

2. "How can we avoid losing focus on the customer while implementing this restructure?"

3. "Is there anything we (or you) can do, in case you have to move, to make things less stressful for your children, or to find a new job for your partner?"

4. "Is there anything we (or you) can do to make taking on a new role easier?"

As a leader, or as an organisation, you can't solve all of the problems. However, you might be able to solve some of them. And, by talking about them, people might get some tips and advice from their colleagues. All of this will help the limbic brain, as well as the rational brain, to be at ease with these changes. And, importantly, you will bring this dialogue into the meeting room, instead of keeping it at the water cooler.

Here is a summary of tool two:

From Decision to Acceptance:

Creating ownership
Whenever you want to implement a solution that is decided by yourself, or someone else higher up or in another department, you can use the following steps:

First, explain the goal of the meeting and how it will go, and then follow the next steps. The goal of the meeting is to see how the change can be implemented, in the way that is most effective and comfortable for your team. This must take place within defined boundaries.

Step one: Ambition

Present the current situation in terms of shocking facts.
Check to make sure everyone understands that these facts are a problem.
Present the ambition in terms of goals to reach.
Check to make sure that everyone sees the importance of the goal.

Step two: Boundaries

Present the solution or change that has to be implemented.
Check to see if there are any concerns. List them, and make sure you understand them.

Step three: Coaching

Find ways to minimise, or to take away, the concerns together.

Your main leadership tool is your own behaviour.

Unknown

Using a simple tool for a complex transformation

When facilitating a leadership conference for the top senior executives of a global company we used a concept we called Plan A and Plan B. These are two very simple and practical tools to get the buy-in of employees. The difference between the two is the starting point. If there is a challenge for which there is not yet a decided solution, then it is wise to use Plan A. It gives us a way of structuring a talk or meeting in order to get buy-in on the challenge, and then also, step-by-step, on the ambition and the playing field. Thereafter, people are given autonomy to find solutions. However, if you have a solution which is already decided, and needs to be implemented, then Plan B is the answer. It helps to transform possible resistance from employees into positive energy that can be used to look for ways to implement the solution in an effective and optimal way. We used and practiced these two tools in the way we usually do, and everything went well. However, a few weeks after the session, we got a call from the HR director asking us if Plan B could also be used to shape a larger change process, and the main kick-off meeting, with a few hundred people. Yes, it was possible, and very effective. They started with announcing the change and its major consequences. Then they formed groups of ten, to exchange concerns and questions. With an app, we made an inventory of all concerns and questions and, during a break, we clustered them into topics to be resolved, in order to make the change happen smoothly. After the break, we organised a World Café, using the topics defined by the employees themselves. We asked them to find ways forward during the World Café but, before starting, we defined the boundaries within which all possible ideas and solutions had to fit. Although the change was not the most popular one, very soon they succeeded in turning possible resistance into creative energy. Employees not only accepted the change, but looked for ways to make it work in the best interests of everyone!

A good tool improves the way you work. A great tool improves the way you think.

Jeff Duntemann

CHAPTER THIRTEEN

So What! Now What? Tips to Shape Your Further Development

Whatever your conclusion is after reading this book, it is always interesting to take the position, "So, what now?"

Whatever the current situation is, it's irrelevant. The only relevant question is how to move forward, and how and where to start. In this last chapter, I want to give you some very practical tips on how to shape your further personal development as a leader.

Start Within 72 Hours

Although sources differ in opinion, there is a consensus that if you want to put what you learn into practice you have to start very soon, preferably within 72 hours of reading this book. If you wait longer than that, your chances of ever putting what you've learned into practice drop to below 30 per cent. So, start immediately by making an action list, putting actions in your agenda, and making the necessary appointments.

Start Small

Never say, "I am going to improve my communication skills." Don't even say, "From now on I am going to ask more questions before I start talking." No, make it small. Limit your scope to a certain skill, in a certain situation, with certain individuals.

For example, "In my weekly talks with Ahmed I am going to ask more reflective questions before I give him overly specific instructions or solutions."

This will help you focus, and Ahmed will be your living reminder.

Bridging the Gap

When you start using your new skills, the most important thing to realise is that, initially, your effectiveness in a conversation will drop. If you want to ask Ahmed reflective questions instead of always giving him the solution or detailed instructions, you will need to think of which questions to ask, rather than trying to get results from the conversation. This may feel like a step backwards. However, if you persevere, you will become a more effective communicator and this behaviour will become automatic. You will have added a skill to your toolbox. It is the gap in effectiveness that you have to bridge. You can do this by creating all kinds of reminders for yourself, so that you don't go back to your old behaviour. You should do this for at least three months.

For example, I knew a CEO who bought a reproduction of a painting by Piet Mondriaan. He put it on the wall opposite his desk so that he could see it behind his conversation partner whenever he was talking with someone in his office. The picture reminded him of the action/reaction tool. So, during every conversation, he was reminded to use the four corners of the Leadership ABCs.

Changing Interaction Patterns

The following story makes clear what it takes to change an interaction pattern between two or more people. The story is about Abena and Christoph, who have been married for several years now. And, of course, what you see is that patterns emerge and they often become fixed.

The pattern between Abena and Christoph is that Christoph often goes out with friends, almost every evening, because Abena argues with him. Abena argues with him a lot because Christoph goes out every evening!

So, if neither of them will take the initiative to change, this pattern will go on forever or until the relationship dissolves.

Imagine that Christoph gains some insight and decides to spend an evening at home. What do you think will happen? There is a big change (because the two are in a pattern) that Abena will use this opportunity to complain even more. She probably thinks that, if she doesn't get her message across that evening, she will never get another chance. Christoph will conclude that staying at home is not working; he will go back to his old behaviour and will go out with friends again. This is often what happens when people try to change an interaction. They try another behaviour, the other doesn't respond as expected, so they conclude that this does not work, and they go back to the old behaviour.

There are two main mechanisms that can improve your chances for successfully breaking interaction patterns. The first is transparency. Tell the other party that you want to change the interaction pattern and that, therefore, you are going to change your own behaviour. In this example, Christoph could have said, "Abena, I see that this is not working for us. I want to change this, so I will stay at home more often."

The second mechanism is even simpler. Specifically, you have to persist! Never expect to change an interaction pattern in a single moment. If Christoph stays at home every evening, the pattern will change and the reason for Abena to complain will no longer exist. The same goes for daily life; when you want to change an interaction, you need to persist!

Postscript: Six Leadership Challenges for the Next Decade

When this book was in its last edit, before being published, I made a new step in my thinking about its different tools and insights, and I found a way to connect the core elements of the New Leadership ABCs to each other. This resulted in a 'how to' leadership pyramid that you can see on my website, www.theleadershippyramid.net

It gives further insights, tools and tips to handle the following leadership challenges:

How to lead the undercurrent
How to lead (hidden) emotions and agendas

Infecting people with purpose
How to infect others with purpose and meaning

Offering solid ground
How to maintain solid ground in times of high volatility

Facilitating productive collaboration
How to structure for optimal collaboration and engagement

Releasing energy
How to get creativity and innovation flowing

Fostering agility
How to become agile

"You cannot predict the outcome of human development. All you can do is like a farmer; create the conditions under which it will begin to flourish."

Ken Robinson

Phases of Child Development and Possible Developmental Drivers of the Ego

There are three major phases of child development until about the age of seven:

1. The first phase is about feeling safe, secure, and nurtured.

2. The second phase is about power and influence: Who determines what I do, and when I do it, others or myself?

3. The third phase is all about having an identity and value within a group of peers. How am I compared to others, and what is my value and position compared to others?

For phase one, I will describe the main emotional themes that play a role, together with some possible strategies a person can use to handle these. A strategy is a fundamental way of turning a drive into an ego (or, as I also call it, your coat). The coat you slowly weave is a way to reconcile, in a consistent way, your inner feelings about the outside world. This coat is a way of creating safety, control, and position. In my estimation, there are as many coats as there are people. A combination of drives can be at work, and a combination of strategies can be used, which always lead to a unique coat.

I hope that, by describing some of the drivers and strategies, I can help you in your self-reflection, and in finding the core of your ambition and drive. It is important to find this core, as often the coat you wove for the past no longer suits you. You might no longer feel comfortable in your coat, without knowing exactly what is wrong. Ambitions related to your coat are not as strong or as important as those coming from your drivers. The drivers and strategies I describe here are drawn from a combination of child development psychology, the Enneagram of Personality, and my own experience.

So, let's have a look at the phases of early development, and the possible drives and related strategies.

The First Phase (Year Zero-One)

In the first phase (year zero-one), it is important that a baby is well nurtured and feels safe and secure. If this is not the case then often feelings of being unsafe and insecure form a core driver, resulting in the development of behaviour to make the world a safer and more predictable place. In the limbic brain, a feeling is created that the world or others are not safe, that they are not there when needed, that they don't fulfil basic needs, that they don't protect, and that they don't hold you when you are afraid. So, one could say that the core driver is to create safety, predictability, and protection for oneself, and often also for others.

This driver can be realised through different strategies of behaviour. One strategy is observing. When a person feels unsafe, one way to resolve this is by keeping quiet and observing very carefully how the world turns; in that way it becomes highly predictable, and therefore safer and more secure. They develop into a quiet, introverted person and a sharp observer, often well educated. The ego you develop, or the coat that you are wearing, is that of an intellectual, preferring to read books instead of interacting with people. If this is the case for you, how real is this ego?

For people on the outside, it might look like this person doesn't have a lot of ambition or passion, but by definition it is there! Look at what this person has done to become this observer. It takes a lot of effort, energy, and focus to become this sharp observer with elaborate ideas on how the world works. This difference between the core passion or energy you feel, and the behavioural strategy that is created to handle this, is crucial. I call it the core driver, and the coat (ego) you have woven is feeding this core driver to protect yourself from the external world.

The second strategy to handle a feeling of a lack of safety is to make yourself part of a bigger whole: to be very loyal to a small or larger group. A small group might be an inner circle of private or professional friends, and a larger group might be a political party, religion, science, or a club. The strategy here is to give and to ask (often demand) loyalty, as a kind of protection. The ego that is presented, or the coat that you are wearing, is that of a loyal person who is always willing to help others within your group.

COAT/EGO: norms, rules, convictions

Appendix Figure 1 Your core driver and your coat/ego

The third strategy to handle a lack of safety and nurturing is denial and avoidance of all unsafe situations. Instead, you focus on the positive and fun side of life. You talk about opportunities instead of dangers. The ego that you present, or the coat that you are wearing, is that of a positive, happy, and joyful person, always ready with a joke or to have some fun.

The Second Phase (Years One-Three)

In the second phase (years one-three), a child becomes more independent and aware of itself, and they begin to understand that they are independent beings, which is when the first conflicts will arise. It is during this period that the limbic brain lays the basis for feelings related to who is in control (me or others), how independent they are, and how allowable it is to have a conflict. If this leads to unresolved issues, then this can be the start of a driver. In this way, you can't say that the core driver is to be in control, or to avoid conflicts.

Here, again, one can see different strategies for handling this driver. The most obvious one is simply to be in control, and to avoid others controlling you. You call the shots, and expect others to follow and recognize you as a leader. The ego that is presented, or the coat that you are wearing, is that of a strong person capable of handling all situations by themselves.

Another strategy is to avoid conflicts and issues related to who is in control. You do this by following others, and you will try to meddle when other people have an argument because it makes you feel uncomfortable. The ego that is presented, or the coat that you are wearing, is that of an amiable person bringing others together and resolving conflicts and arguments.

The last strategy I want to describe is that of adopting a strong set of norms, often those of your parents, that dictate your understanding of how the world works. Strong norms, values, and rules allow you to avoid conflict and discussion. The ego that is presented, or the coat that you are wearing, is that of a person with an enormous sense of responsibility because of your strong set of rules and norms. If everyone would follow the same rules and norms, then conflict would not arise; they would dictate what needs to happen so any question about who calls the shots is no longer relevant.

The Third Phase (Years Six-Seven)

In the third phase (years six-seven), children are more and more in contact with their peers. Issues and themes that come into play during this period concern: Who am I in relation to my peers? Do I have value compared to others? Can I build a sense of my own identity? In the limbic brain, feelings about identity and self-awareness are created. So, one could say that the core driver is to build a sense of self or position compared to peers, and to build one's own identity.

The first strategy to tackle this is to help others. Taking care of others gives you a feeling of usefulness, a clear role in the group, and an identity of caretaker. The ego that is presented, or the coat that you are wearing, is that of a person who is sensitive to the needs of others and is always willing to help and support.

The second strategy is to show how capable you are. You will create a sense of identity and self-value by being very competent at something and by trying to outperform others in this field. Often you become competitive and are probably also a high achiever. The ego that is presented, or the coat that you are wearing, is that of a capable, self-confident person, able to perform and get results.

The last strategy to handle this driver is to label yourself as special and different from others. You create self-value and identity by defining yourself as a special individual, which is also why it is difficult for you to be part of a peer group. Things that are mainstream are not for you. Everything has to be special, often very creative, and exceptional. The ego that is presented, or the coat that you are wearing, is that of a creative, original individual, clearly different from the mainstream.

This chart provides an overview of key drivers, and how they translate into different personality types. It also explores what the common traps are for each type, how it might inspire specific professional ambitions, and what the key lessons are to avoid falling into negative patterns.

CORE DRIVER	STRATEGY	EGO/COAT
Creating safety and predictability.	Observing and predicting.	An intellectual, preferring to read books instead of interacting with other people.
	Offering and asking for loyalty.	Someone that is loyal to others, and thus helpful and accountable.
	Denying unsafe or unpleasant situations.	A positive, happy, and joyful person, always ready with a joke or to have some fun.
Being in control or avoiding conflict.	Being in control, and calling the shots.	A strong person, capable of handling all situations by themselves.
	Avoiding conflict and issues of being in control.	An amiable person, bringing others together and resolving conflicts and arguments.
	Adopting a strong set of norms.	A person with an enormous sense of responsibility, following a strong set of rules and norms.
Creating an identity.	Helping others.	A person sensitive to the needs of others, and always willing to help and support.
	Performing.	A capable, self-confident person, able to perform and get results.
	Being special.	A creative, original individual, clearly different from the mainstream.

TRAP	HOW DRIVER IS TRANSLATED INTO PROFESSIONAL AMBITIONS	TO LEARN
Getting disconnected from people, and therefore feeling less safe.	Developing high-level concepts and technology.	That the world is not that unsafe.
To lose yourself and your own needs in your loyalty towards others.	Developing high-level and dependable products, models, and a culture of loyalty.	That other people are not unsafe.
Not able to see the potential for problems and thus creating unpleasant situations.	Creating fun, joy, positivity, and comfort.	That negative feelings of pain and frustration can be very positive.
By always wanting to be in control, one can lose control.	Goals and ambitions that require action and getting results.	You will not be overtaken when not always in control.
When avoiding conflict, one is avoiding and losing oneself.	Goals and ambitions that please, reconcile, and don't cause any problems.	That conflict can be positive and fruitful.
Becoming a slave to your own norms.	High-quality products and services, and high integrity.	To loosen up. Nothing happens when norms become a bit less strict once in a while.
Helping others is finally not producing a sense of self-value.	Service and client intimacy.	Taking into account own needs.
Becoming too competitive, so that connection with others is lost and image is too important.	Slick and fashionable products and services.	That performing is not the only way to be someone.
Getting more and more disconnected from others, and placing yourself outside the group.	Innovation, creativity, being different, and having unique selling points.	Recognize that you are a human being like everyone else.

Acknowledgements

First of all, I want to thank the source of my life, my parents Jozef Vanschoenwinkel and Adeline Coninx. Together with my two elder brothers, Tony and Jean Vanschoenwinkel, they laid the foundation of who I am today and of my accomplishments.

During my studies as a clinical psychologist, there was a great man that forever influenced my mind and shaped my thinking in a way for which I am truly grateful. It was Professor Dr. Jean-Pierre De Waele.

When I started my career there were two people who supported me and who I considered to be my professional parents. They educated me in a setting of high professionalism and integrity. So, I say thanks to Christine and Maurice Sleypen.

Several colleagues come to mind who so often gave me a positive vibe and always supported me to believe in my own talents. I don't think they realize the immense effect they had on my personal development just by believing in me, being there and giving advice: Jolande Koolen, Marieke Borleffs, Clemens Wubbels, Joke Steenhagen, Facila Nanhekhan, Maartje Van Boekholt, Marloes Luiten, and so many others.

A special thanks to Nicolien Dellensen, as she was the first to give me structural feedback about this book, and who radiated a belief that this would be a valuable document.

To Carel Maasland, as he was the source of so many opportunities, and a great inspiration in the field of ambitious people management.

Also, a very special thanks to my business partners, who are also friends that walked alongside me in my professional career: Herman, Govert, and Marlies.

Herman Sweldens, with whom I gave birth to Teasing Consult in Belgium, I want to thank for his positivity, enthusiasm and faith to sail along.

I am very grateful to Govert van Sandwijk for the enormous impact he has had on my personal and professional development. His never decreasing faith in my talent and professionalism has led to accomplishments I would have never imagined.

Marlies Zeeuwen, I not only thank for years of support, reflection and great collaboration, but even more so for the personal enrichment and development this brought me.

Thanks also to Erik Dirven for his input and inspiration on change and transformation management.

A ton of gratitude goes out to all the people that allowed me to touch their lives within training coaching and facilitation. In turn, they cannot imagine how they touched mine.

Big thanks to all of the people who made this book possible in a practical way: Brian Baker (structural editing), Sarah Busby(copy editing and proofreading), Jason Anscomb (cover design), Shaun Loftus (marketing), J-P Stanway (internal design) and Stan de Wijs (website design).

And, last but far from least, gratitude and blessings to my dear friend Piet Geris for a lifetime of support.

Bibliography

Amen, D., Change Your Brain, Change Your Life: The Breakthrough Programme for Conquering Anger, Anxiety, Obsessiveness and Depression, Piatkus. 2010

Bateson, G., Mind and Nature: A Necessary Unity, Hampton Press, cop. 2002.

Blekkingh, B., Authentic leadership: Discover and Live Your Essential Mission, Oxford Infiniteideas. 2015

Collins, J., Good to Great: Why Some Companies Make the Leap and Others Don't, HarperCollins 2011

Dilts, R., Sleight of Mouth: The Magic of Conversational Belief Change, Meta Publications 1999

Goleman, D., Emotional intelligence: Why It Can Matter More Than IQ, Bloomsbury. 2005

Hofstede G. et al, Cultures and Organisations: Software of the Mind: Intercultural Cooperation and its Importance for Survival, McGraw-Hill. 2010

van Hooff, J., Gebiologeerd, Spectrum. 2019

Johnson et al, Fundamentals of Strategy, Pearson. 2018

Johnson et al, Exploring Corporate Strategy, FT/Prentice Hall. 2005

Leary, T., Interpersonal Diagnosis of Personality: A Functional Theory and Methodology for Personality Evaluation, Resource Publications. 2004

O'Keeffe, A., Hardwired Humans: Successful Leadership Using Human

Instincts, Roundtable Press. 2011

Pink, D., Drive: The Surprising Truth About What Motivates Us, Canongate Books. 2018

Rock, D. & Page, L., Coaching with the Brain in Mind: Foundations for Practice, John Wiley & Sons. 2009

Taylor, F. W., The Principles of Scientific Management, CreateSpace Independent Publishing Platform. 2011

Vandendriessche, F. et al, Leading Without Commanding, Output Academy. 2006

Vermeren, P., Rondom Leiderschap, Terra Lannoo. 2014

de Waal, F., Are We Smart Enough to Know How Smart Animals Are?, W.W. Norton & Company. 2016

De Waele, J. P, Les Cas Programmés en Criminologie, Mardaga. 1995